The Journey

Jess Sweely

Acorn Hill Press—Madison, VA
ISBN: 979-8-218-14001-4
Library of Congress Control Number: 2023901654
Title: *The Journey*
Author: Jess Sweely
Digital distribution | 2023
Paperback | 2023

Dedication

This book is dedicated to my wife, Sharon, who has been my partner and support for over 60 years and for which I would not have been able to achieve my goals without her by my side. I also want to thank all those who have mentored me over the years. Without them, I would not be who I am today.

Chapter One

In November of 1961, I was hired as a junior accountant in Main & Co.'s, Washington, D.C. office. Main & Co. Was a Certified Public Accounting firm who claimed to be the 10th largest in the United States. The consensus among Certified Public Accounting firms then, was that there were eight major firms (the "Big Eight").

I majored in accounting in college, but I still had no idea of what was involved in working for a C.P.A. firm. How did I get to this turn in the road? As Paul Harvey would say, "Now the rest of the story."

I was born May 28, 1938 in Clearfield, Pa. to Elmer and Elizabeth Shope Sweely. My family, on both my mother and father's side, worked for the New York Central Railroad and had for at least three generations. My mother and father had 10th grade educations. They had to quit school to earn a living during the great depression. My father's ancestry was mostly German (Schwelles) and my mother's was mostly German &Scot- Irish (Shope & Boyle).

In 2016 both Sharon and I took an ancestry DNA test. I was found to be 72.3% Irish, Scottish & Welsh; 24% Scandinavian; 2.9% Greek and 0.8% American Indian. Sharon was found to be 59.8% English; 37.5 % Scandinavian 2.7% Eastern European.

We both thought we had more German ancestry but who knows. The Greek and American Indian was a surprise.

My father was the oldest of seven children (born in 1901), and my mother was in the middle of six children (born 1918). Only my father's younger brother, Fred, was fortunate to attend college. He received an athletic scholarship to Dickinson College in 1918 where he lettered in football, basketball and track & field. He went on to get his Master's in Education at Pennsylvania State University (Penn State) and was in education all his life. He finished his career as the Clearfield County Superintendent of Schools.

Clearfield is in Central Pennsylvania and was and is a blue collar working class area. The major industries in the 1940's and 50's were strip mining for coal, railroads to haul the coal to larger cities and brick and sewer pipe production because of the clay deposits in the area.

Those industries are all gone today. Clearfield had a population of about 9,300 in the 1950's. Today the population is around 5,300. This reduction is the result of the industries downsizing or closing altogether. Clearfield is located on the West Branch of the Susquehanna.

It wasn't easy traveling out of Central Pennsylvania in the 1950's as there were no interstate highways and no passenger train service. The Trailway's Bus Company did operate a limited schedule in Central Pennsylvania.

Pittsburgh was a little over 100 miles away but it could take 3 or more hours to get there. Philadelphia was even further away and there wasn't any obvious reason for anyone to go there.

My father was a master mechanic on the New York Central Railroad. He was trained to rebuild and repair the steam locomotives that were fueled by coal and later oil. He worked between Clearfield, Cherry Tree, Jersey Shore and Williamsport. Clearfield and Jersey Shore and Williamsport had "turntables" where the train engines could be placed and then rotated to one of the bays in the "round house" where work could be performed. I visited my Dad often when he was working to bring lunch.

We lived in Jersey Shore, Pa. until I was around 5, then we moved to Cherry Tree, Pa. I started school in Cherry Tree and went through the 5th grade there. We moved back to Clearfield went I was 11 and I went to grades 6 through 12 in Clearfield schools. Clearfield, Cherry Tree, Jersey Shore and Williamsport, Pa. were all major employment areas for the New York Central Railroad. The freight trains took coal from Central Pa. to other east coast locations. There were no passenger trains on this line.

Cherry Tree had a population of approximately 500 people in 1944. Today it is closer to 350...all sewage when into the West Branch of the Susquehanna River. As a result the central water that most homes had was not drinkable. There was a central well on a hill overlooking Cherry Tree. The well had a hand pump and the entire population of the town used this well for their water. Everyone had milk cans that they would fill up and take home. The only industry was the railroad.

Indiana, Clearfield and Cambria counties came together at Cherry Tree where the head waters of the West Branch of the Susquehanna and Cushion Creek come together. There was a monument there to honor William Penn and a small dam at this location.

There wasn't a lot to keep one busy in this small railroad town. In the summer we went fishing and swimming in the creek at the monument where William Penn had come and where the three counties came together.

School was in one building for all 12 grades. First through third grade was in one classroom taught by one teacher. The same was true for grades four through six. Starting in seventh grade, each grade had one teacher and their own room.

The teacher would start with one grade and then give them an assignment and then move to the second grade and then the third grade. Sometimes she would address all three grades at the same time.

I am a natural left hander but in those days everyone had to be right handed in school. I was cracked with a pointer more than once on my knuckles and told to use my right hand to write. At the front of the room, mounted on a nail, was a paddle with holes. This was used by the teacher for discipline. If you were disciplined at school you knew you would get another whipping when you got home.

On Saturday, in the fall, I would curl up in a chair at home, next to a radio, and listen to the Notre Dame Football games and pretend that I was Notre Dame's quarterback, Johnny Lujack.

Clearfield had a number of "out houses" in the late 1940's and a number of us kids would go "tipping" at Halloween. We would also stand in front of the school, behind trees, and when a car would go by we would throw a pumpkin into the air to land on the car. This was fun until one on the cars was the local police chief. He stopped and we ran but he caught us and gave us a good chewing out, took our names and said he would be talking to our parents. Thank goodness he didn't but we were done with our outing pranks.

We moved to Clearfield in 1949 where I entered the sixth grade. This was a new experience. Clearfield had a population of about 9,300 with three elementary schools, one junior high (Grades 7-9) and one high school (Grades 10-12). It also had a separate Catholic School System. In addition the town had three movie theatres, a library, and a central shopping area.

This was the first time that I had the opportunity to participate in team sports. I joined a Little League Baseball team in 1950.

My folks were insistent that I get good grades in school and make the honor role. If not, I had to answer when report cards came out. When I started junior high school I was primarily interested in sports. In high school, I was on the football, baseball, volleyball and basketball teams and really hadn't thought much beyond that. I did keep my grades up but I lived from day to day.

Clearfield had a downtown area with bus service to the East End, West Side and Uptown.

The East End, where I lived, was made up of mostly blue collar working folks. It bordered the Sewer Plant, Brick Yard and Railroad yards. It was predominately Italian. Most of my friend's grandparents only spoke Italian as they had come over from the "old country."

The uptown area was made up of professionals, doctors, lawyers and business types. The West Side was on the east side of the Susquehanna River. It was also where the hospital with its nursing school was located and the "Driving Park" where sports events were held as well as the annual "County Fair."

There was a YMCA in the center of town. It was the focal point for most after school activities. I spent many hours at the "Y." My mother often threatened to pack a bag and send it to the Y because I spent so much time there.

I also joined a local Boy Scout Troup, Troup 2, and I eventually reached the rank of Eagle Scout. I was also selected for and initiated into "The Order of the Arrow."

One of the projects that I participated in was a Civil Aviation program that tracked all aircraft over the United States.

In the early 1950's there was apparent concern that the Russians might send their aircraft to the United States. This was the era of the "Cold War." As a result the United States, through Civil Aviation, set up a system to monitor all aircraft 24/7. As a result my scout troop participated. The highest building in town was the Dimeling Hotel. I believe it was about 6 stories high. The roof had a shed that had a phone that was connected directly to a monitoring station in Pittsburgh, Pa.

There were pictures of both U S and Russian aircraft on the wall. If you heard an aircraft you were to try to identify it and pick up the phone and tell the Pittsburgh station the type and what direction it was travelling. If you couldn't identify it you would say, "unidentified aircraft flying" and the direction. For approximately two years I manned this location with someone else for 4 hours a week. Others from the area manned it the remaining time.

Looking back, this was a stupid thing to be doing. In that era, there was no way that the Russians had aircraft that could have reached the United States. Again, a product of the cold war.

These activities tended to keep you on the straight and narrow and out of trouble.

I worked different jobs to earn spending money from the age of 12 until I graduated from high school. My first job was carrying the local Clearfield paper, "The Progress." When I was 15, I worked one summer in in a local potato chip company making potato chips.

When I was 16 and had my driver's license, I delivered groceries for Petuill's, our local neighborhood market. Folks would call their grocery order in and I would deliver it. I also worked in the store stocking the shelves and at the close of business I had to clean and scrap the butcher block with a steel brush.

When I was 17, I worked one summer as an electrician's helper on the New York Central Railroad in Williamsport, Pa. where my father was working. We stayed in the bunkhouse at the railroad yard during the week and came home on weekends. This was a true learning experience as I interacted with a variety of folks. The man that ran the bunkhouse and the restaurant was from Greece and we became friends.

He had purchased a home that had an attic full of old books. He asked me if I would like them because he had no need for them. I took them and still have a few today. Most were burned in a fire that we had in our attic in Clearfield.

I was in the last class (1956) that graduated from the old high school in downtown Clearfield. I applied to Penn State and was accepted and entered as a freshman in the fall of 1956. I thought that I wanted to study Pre-Med but I soon realized that this wasn't my calling. I started to take some business classes and came to the realization that these classes were more to my liking. Beginning my second year at Penn State I worked at the Hetzel Union Building (HUB) for meals. I later joined The Pi Kappa Alpha Fraternity.

During the summer between my freshman and sophomore year at Penn State, I worked at the local Harbison-Walker Brickyard. I was one of three summer students assigned to maintain their railroad right-a-way. This was a dirty, nasty, backbreaking job. We repaired rails and ties on the brick yards right- a -way. The rails weighted about 1,000 pounds and the ties about 200 pounds. We used what looked like an ice tong to move them. Our supervisor was a wily old retired railroad track boss, Johnny Celo. He taught us how to pound spikes into the ties, and to hold the rail in place, using our legs instead of just our arms. He also taught us that we had to work together to maximize the amount of work achieved. Safety measures were always number one. Many life lessons were learned from this experience.

My last month at the brickyard I was assigned to the silo's where clay was stored. The clay moved by a conveyor belt at the bottom of the silo to where it automatically went into molds for firebrick. I didn't realize it then, but this was a very dangerous job. My job was to keep the clay from gathering on the sides of the silo. OSHA regulations wouldn't allow you to be in the silo today.

The one thing that I didn't realize at the time was that I was learning a work ethic as well as teamwork. Responsibility, being on time and doing a good job were critical items in a working environment.

My newspaper route consisted of about 100 papers, six days a week, after school. I earned 5 cents per paper per week or about $5.00 a week. This was a big deal to a 12 year old kid. A haircut was 25 cents and a movie was 19 cents. With 50 cents I could get a haircut, go to the movie; buy a piece of candy and have a penny leftover.

I made 50 cents an hour at the potato chip factory; I think the railroad paid $1.85 an hour and the brick yard about $1.25 an hour. The railroad was a union job and even though I wasn't in the union they paid me union wages.

After working at the brickyard, I knew that if I were ever to achieve something other than working at a manual labor job I needed to get an education. Manual labor was not what I envisioned for my future.

One of the benefits which my father had working for the New York Central Railroad was free travel for himself and his family. We didn't take vacations but because of the railroad pass we were able to travel to New York City where two of my father's sisters lived.

They were both married. One lived in Belmont and the other in Jamaica on Long Island, outside of New York City. Using my father's railroad pass, we visited them in the summer of 1953 and 1954.

We had to drive to Altoona, Pa. where we would board a passenger train that would take us to Philadelphia via Harrisburg. At Philadelphia we would change trains and get on a train to New York. The train to Philadelphia was steam, coal fired, and when you got off you had soot everywhere.

There was no such thing as air conditioning then. You had to have the windows open and the soot came into everything.

The train from Philadelphia to New York was electric. The total trip would take over 14 hours. We would be met at Penn Station in New York by one of my Uncle's.

One of my Uncle's, Bill Glynn, had emigrated from Ireland and worked as a Payroll Supervisor for Lever Brothers. My other Uncle, Fred Nightingale, was a manager for the U.S. Department of Agriculture. He was from Clearfield and had received a degree in horticulture from Penn State.

During those visits, we went into New York City and saw baseball games at the Dodger's Ebbetts Field and the Giant's Polo Grounds. We also went to Ellis Island, the Statue of Liberty, Coney Island and Jones Beach.

This exposure was so different from anything that I could ever have imagined. Central Pennsylvania had nothing to compare to this. It was almost overwhelming. It made you realize that there was a new and different world outside of Central Pennsylvania, different than anything one could imagine. I also realized that an education was necessary in order to move forward.

As I entered high school in 1953, our teachers talked to us about what our plans were for after high school. My Senior Class consisted of approximately 225 young people. Some were planning to go into the service, some were going to work on the family farms, some were planning to go to college and others were going to work in the trades. I would estimate that about 10 to 15% were going to college.

We had a college preparatory track in high school and also a vocational education track for the trades. I was told from an early age on that I was going to college. My folks did not have the opportunity to go but they wanted that for me.

I had no idea what I wanted to do. One Christmas when I was 10 or 11, I received a Doctor's kit. I decided then that I would be a Doctor. I didn't know what was involved but that was my plan.

Career advisors in high school were not very helpful. I think that teachers in the 1950's were dedicated and wanted to be teachers but they were not in a position to advise someone of the various opportunities that existed in the "real world." I am not sure that it is any difference today.

The summer that I graduated from high school, I was playing baseball for the Clearfield Mountain League Team. The Pittsburgh Pirates team came to our area to have tryouts for their franchise. I was selected for the tryouts. I had always played first base but during the tryouts they asked me to try left field. I wasn't tall enough to be a first baseman but they thought the outfield might be a possibility since I was a good hitter and had a decent arm.

Everything went well until they timed us running the bases. I wasn't fast enough and any future in baseball ended.

In the 1950's, Pennsylvania had a large number of State Teachers Colleges. Today they have been converted to colleges or universities. I didn't plan to be a teacher so these were not an option. Penn State was a State University and only about 45 miles away. I decided that I would apply there. I didn't apply anywhere else because cost was a factor. I think Penn State was required to accept all state students if they met the admissions standard.

I was accepted and admitted to the Pre-Med program. I had taken the college prep course in high school and thought I was ready. What a surprise I was in for. Most of my fellow students had advanced math and sciences courses in high school while I had only the basics.

In September 1956, I matriculated at Penn State University in State College, Pa. Penn State had about 10,000 students. The town's population was about the same. This was a huge culture shock.

My roommate was from Pittsburgh and he was also in Pre-Med. He was so much better prepared for college than I was.

It soon became obvious that Pre-Med wasn't for me. The chemistry and math courses were so advanced over what I had taken in high school. The students from the Pittsburgh and Philadelphia area were so far ahead because they had more advanced courses in the sciences and math then we had.

Penn State also had a moto of "education for the masses." They were pioneering the use of Close- Circuit TV for many of their courses. This allowed them to reach more students with fewer faculty. As an example, I had CCTV courses in chemistry, economics, accounting, ROTC, and transportation among others.

A class could easily have 200 or 300 students. They would have multiple rooms with two or three TV sets in the room and about 25 students. There was a graduate student and a monitor at the front of the room. The graduate student had a console at the front of the room which had a button that could be pushed and the Professor could see from his monitor. He could ignore it or take a question.

More times than not, you would be ignored because the Professor had so much material to cover that questions were hardly ever taken. Also, you never knew whether the lectures were live or taped. Usually one class a week would be with a graduate assistant. Most of this time was spent discussing what had been presented in previous CCTV class.

There was little or no interaction with the Professor. Not an acceptable way to learn. This was an alternative to large classes of 200 to 250 students in an auditorium taught by one person.

After the first semester I knew that I had to change majors. One of my schoolmates suggested that I take an accounting course. I had no idea what accounting was but I found that I had an aptitude for accounting and finance. I wasn't certain how all of this went together but I found a new area that seemed to fit me.

Penn State was a "Land Grant School" and as such all male students were required to take two years of compulsory ROTC. I selected Air Force ROTC and subsequently joined the Air Force Pershing Rifle Association, a drill team.

As part of our education we were taken on trips to various Air Force bases to experience an actual active duty Air Force facility. We went on a C-47 aircraft with bucket seats along the sides and parachutes for everyone. We visited Stewart Air Force Base in New York and Eglin Air Force Base in Florida. This exposure was invaluable in my growth and understanding of how the world operated. I decided that I would apply for the Advanced ROTC program and attempt to make the Air Force a career.

Later, when I took my first commercial flight on an Allegheny DC-3 aircraft from Black Moshannon Airport to Washington, D.C., I was surprised that there were no parachutes on board. I had been conditioned that when you flew that you had on a parachute. I was sitting next to Congressman James E. Van Zandt of Pennsylvania. He was the Congressman from my District who would later give me an alternate appointment to the U.S. Air Force Academy. He said that I should relax and everything would be fine. He was right!

During my third semester at Penn State I was invited to join the Pi Kappa Alpha Fraternity. I moved into the fraternity house at the beginning of my fourth semester. The monthly cost was $90.00 a month and that included room and board. Living with others from all over Pennsylvania was a new experience.

Some of the fraternity members were majoring in engineering, business, architecture, meteorology, and many others. This experience exposed me to a new world of young men with experiences very different then what I was accustomed to. It further helped me to see the world that existed outside of Central Pennsylvania and one that I would eventually become part of.

I was accepted into the Air Force Advanced ROTC program after my sophomore year, providing I passed the final physical scheduled for August of 1958. I had also received an appointment to the Air Force Academy at the same time as an alternate. There was a good chance that I would be able to move up and be accepted. That physical was also scheduled for the same time period.

I was going to summer school in 1958 to make up some of the courses that I needed after switching majors. I caught a ride back to school with a friend one week-end in July 1958.

We were within 6 miles of State College when we topped a hill and saw a car stalled across both lanes of traffic. My friend swerved to the right and hit the rear corner of the car and we went into a ditch and the car flipped over. I flew out of the car and somehow the car came down on top of me. My friend was also thrown out. He slid about a hundred feet down the highway. He suffered only some abrasions but I suffered a broken femur bone. Fortunately, I landed in a ditch. That saved me from more intensive injuries as the car had landed on top of my leg.

State College did not have a hospital in the 1950's. The closest hospital was in Bellefonte, Pa. about 10 miles away. I was taken there by ambulance and upon arriving I was stabilized. Dr. Locke, an orthopedic surgeon, was called in. Dr. Locke was in his 60's but was their top orthopedic surgeon.

After evaluating me and looking at the x-rays he told me that he would operate but not until the swelling went down. He would then insert a metal rod into the marrow of my femur bone to hold the two parts in place. I would have to have it in for about 12 months, after which they would remove it. They would use a bit and brace to drill a hole in the upper part of the femur bone and then hammer it in to the lower piece.

This technique had been perfected by the Germans in World War II. Many of our airmen had suffered broken femurs bailing out over Germany when their aircraft were shot down. This technique worked well and allowed many to walk immediately.

Within a few days, the swelling had gone down enough to operate. The operation was successful but I had to spend almost a month in the hospital before I was allowed to go home. I was told that they almost lost me during the operation. I do remember a huge black hole and being dragged into it.

I was on crutches for almost 6 months and then I used a cane for another 3 to 4 months. My Air Force ROTC plans were now over as I could not take the physical. I went back to school on crutches but I was like a boat without a compass. I had no idea where I was going and what I was going to do.

Growing up in Clearfield, I attended St. John's Lutheran Church. The pastor was Dr. E. Roy Hauser. I admired him and had been counseled in church teachings. I went to him to discuss my situation. He told me that all things would come into focus if I believed. He was correct.

In the summer of 1959 I had the rod removed at the Clearfield Hospital. The first try wasn't successful as I was in a different hospital and they didn't have the right tools. After the incisions healed and the doctors got the right tools I was in for a second try. This time they were successful.

My parents had contacted a local attorney, William Chase, concerning the accident. He was successful in getting a settlement from the insurance carrier in the amount of $6,000. My parents gave me a check for $3,000 and kept the other $3,000.

My Uncle Fred, a horticulturist and Department of Agriculture employee had now been relocated to the main office of the Department of Agriculture in Washington D.C. He suggested that I should relocate to Northern Virginia and stay with them while I tried to sort out what my next step would be.

I decided, if I wanted to move on, that might be the best approach. My mother and father thought that it made sense and so I left home for good.

A new adventure and where would it lead?

My uncle and aunt lived in North Springfield, VA. and I became part of their family. They had two girls, Jane and Nancy, my cousins. I became like their older brother. My Uncle counseled me and I started to look forward to what life might bring. I had an aptitude for accounting but I needed to finish school and get a degree.

Jess Sweely's childhood home

Maternal grandparents – Halford and Jeannie Shope

Fraternal Grandparents- Jess & Emma Sweely

Father - Elmer Sweely -Front 4th from Right

Uncle Fred & Aunt Doris Nightingale & Jess Oct 7, 1961

Jess - Graduation High School 1956

Chapter Two
American Security & Trust

Jess -US Army 1960

The first thing that I needed was a job. I found a job at a bank very quickly. I was hired as a teller at American Security and Trust and was sent to their Capital Hill Branch at 9th and East Capital Street. Although small, this branch handled the banking for many of the employees on Capitol Hill.

One of my customers was Bobby Baker and his wife. Bobby Baker was the infamous assistant to Lyndon Johnson who was then Senator Pro-Tempore. Bobby Baker was implicated in the Continental Connector scandal.

I found a roommate and we rented rooms in a private home in McLean, VA. My roommate was going to night school at Benjamin Franklin University, an accounting and business school located at 16th and L Street in Washington. I applied and was accepted into their night program.

The branch of American Security that I was assigned to had a Branch Manager, a Note Teller and two other tellers. It was an active location and we were busy all day. The bank hours were 9:00 A.M. to 2:00 P.M. We were slated to arrive by 8:00 A.M. We didn't reopen after we closed at 2:00 P.M... We were able to leave as soon as we had balanced out our teller tray. I was paid at a weekly rate of $65.00 a week or $3,380 per year. In 2016 dollars that would amount to about $27,000 today. In addition one of the fringe benefits was a free checking account.

I had about $200,000 in my teller tray, mostly $500 and $1,000 bills. This was not unusual then, but would be considered outrageous today.

I found that I was usually checked out by 3:00 P.M. and since classes didn't start until 6:00 P.M. I would go to the Library of Congress for a few hours of study before classes. The Library was only 9 blocks from the bank so it was an easy stop.

I had my nest egg of $3,000 and talked to the branch manager about investing in the stock market. He arraigned for me to meet a broker at Merrill Lynch Pierce Fenner & Smith. They were one of the largest brokerage firms in the nation. I met with the broker and he wanted to know what my objectives were. I said that I was hoping to grow my funds. He said that he would make some suggestions but he felt I should consider solid companies with good track records. I left it up to him.

A few months later I had a customer who knew I was invested in the stock market. He came in one day and suggested that I should take any funds that I had available and buy stock in a company called Haloid-Xerox. I asked him what they did and he said that they made copying machines. He handed me an annual report and said that this was going to be the next "big thing." I had no idea at the time what a copy machine was.

I read the report and saw that they predicted that the copying machine was going to revolutionize the world. At the time, if you wanted a copy of something, you had to use copy paper when typing and it could be a mess. Haloid-Xerox had 98 employees and was based in Rochester, NY.

I called my broker and asked him about the company. He said that the stock was at about $30.00 a share but he felt that it was too speculative. I asked him how much cash did we have? He said around $300.00, so I told him to buy 10 shares. This was one of the best decisions I ever made. The stock started to move upward and split a few times. I sold it, just before getting married in 1961, for something around $3,000. The company was listed on the New York Stock Exchange in July 1961 and the stock was in demand. I used the proceeds to buy an engagement ring for Sharon and to furnish our first apartment. I have always wondered what that stock would be worth if I had kept it. I did look one time and decided it was better not knowing.

Former schoolmates of our Branch Manager controlled the "numbers" in Washington, DC and the slot machines in Southern Maryland. Every day, Mike, the numbers man would bring in a paper bag with $1.00 bills and I would exchange them for $500 or $1,000 bills. He would bring in about $10,000 daily. This was 1959.

The slot machine mogul would bring in his change daily, already rolled. I would convert it to mostly $50 and $100 bills, His take was about half of the numbers take.

This wasn't supposed to be done but the Branch Manager and the other two had grown up together.

I also had control of the coin inventory that was in the safe. That amounted to about $50,000.

You had to be 21 to work as a teller. One of the employees, Bob, was a mail teller. He was only 19. His job was to open the mail (many folks sent deposits by mail) reconcile the deposits and give them to one of the regular tellers to put in their daily work.

The regular teller was supposed to reconcile the deposits before putting them in their work. However, this wasn't always the case. You would accept that it was correct and if not, you would not be able to balance out at the end of the day.

Bob was married even though he was only 19. He and his wife had an apartment close to downtown Washington in Arlington, VA. On Friday nights he started to have poker games at his apartment and he would broil steaks and serve dinner.

I started going to the poker games but I felt bad because I was winning $40 to $60 a week, almost as much as my salary. Bob wouldn't take any money for dinner so after a while I decided to stop going because I felt bad for him. I wondered how he could afford to continue this as he always lost.

A month or so after I stopped going to the games, one of my customers came to my teller window with their bank statement and said that one of their mail deposits hadn't been recorded. I took her over to the Bank Manager so that he could determine what had happened.

A few months after, I had a person come to my teller window and show me an FBI badge and ask to talk to me. I called the Bank Manager over and he said to go into the break room at the back of the bank.

The FBI agent indicated that he wanted to ask me some questions about Bob.

Bob hadn't been to work for a few days and we all assumed he was sick.

The FBI agent knew about the Friday evening poker games and proceeded to ask me how the mail deposits were handled.

Apparently Bob had been kiting the mail deposits and that is what had happened to the customer that didn't get her deposit recorded. This had been going on for some time. Many of the deposits had cash in them and he would take the cash and at a later date put that deposit through with a check from someone else that matched the amount of the deposit. The FBI had Bob in custody. I was designated to be a witness at his trial. On the day of his trial he pled guilty and so I wasn't required to testify.

I felt bad for his wife. I don't know how much he had stolen but it was apparently a significant amount.

From that time on mail deposits were distributed to various tellers. This way no one person had control over them.

I worked as a teller from August 1959 through June 1960. I graduated from Benjamin Franklin University in May of 1960 and upon graduation, I was again eligible for the military draft. I realized that I no longer wanted to make a career in the military but I had an obligation to serve.

Military Service

Prior to graduating from Benjamin Franklin, I decided to join the Virginia National Guard. I was assigned to the Niki Ajax Missile Defense Battery that was located in Fairfax, Virginia, off of Rt. 123.

The Cold War was still in full force and Washington and Baltimore were surrounded with "hot" Nike Ajax Missile Defense sites. These were manned by full time National Guard personnel and supplemented by part- time Guardsmen. They reported to a Command Center located at Fort Meade in Maryland. These Nike Ajax missile sites were live sites. The Nike missiles had a range of approximately 25 miles.

Upon joining the Virginia National Guard I had to go on active duty for 6 months of basic training and advanced training on the Niki Ajax missile. I was then required to spend 7 ½ years in the active reserves.

I graduated from Benjamin Franklin University with a B.C.S. degree in June of 1960 and on July 16th I was on a troop train from Alexandria, VA. to Fort Knox, Kentucky for Army Basic Training. Since I had been in ROTC at Penn State, I was chosen to be a Trainee Platoon Sergeant during basic training. During basic training I was asked to consider changing my status to regular Army and go to Officer Candidate School, to become an officer. I gave some consideration to this but decided that I had missed that window of opportunity with my automobile accident. My path was now to satisfy my military obligation and return to the civilian work force.

I finished basic training in mid-September 1960 and was then sent to Fort Bliss, Texas for advance training on the Nike Ajax Missile System. On December 21st my advanced missile defense training was completed and I was released back to my National Guard Unit.

Our Texas battalion consisted of 18 year olds just out of high school and 22 and 23 year olds just out of college.

One of my close friends, Jerry Schwartz, had graduated from the University of Delaware with a degree in Accounting and had a job waiting for him with Price Waterhouse, a large C.P.A. firm in Los Angeles. He tried to convince me that I should come with him and that I would be able to find a job in Los Angeles. I considered it but decided that I needed to return to Washington, D.C. Jerry went on to pass his CPA exam and start his own entertainment accounting firm which became very successful. I sometimes wonder what would have happened if I had gone with him.

Another member of our group was Ed Hume. Ed had graduated from Oberlin College. Ed was a writer and became very successful writing TV and Movie screenplays. Ralph Rabbinowitz was also another member of our group.

Ralph was an attorney, having passed the Bar Exam after his Junior Year at the University of Virginia. Ralph went on to have his own Admiralty Law Firm in Norfolk, VA.

Ralph related a story that is probably as plausible today as then. Between his second and third year of law school he worked in New York City at a large law firm as an intern. When he arrived to go to work, they gave him an office and told him he would receive a phone call. He received a call from a partner, who gave him an assignment. The assignment lasted for the summer and Ralph wrote a legal brief and turned it in. He never met the partner or any associates during his time there. At completion of the summer he was offered a permanent position for when he graduated from law school.

Obviously, he turned the offer down.

Fort Bliss was an open post and our barracks were close to the main highway. Across the highway was Biggs Air Force Base. It was a Strategic Air Command Base and had B-52's that were always on stand-by with nuclear weapons.

On week-ends we would get a pass and go to Juarez, Mexico to the Bull Fights. As I recall, it was cheaper to sit in the sunny side then the shady side of the stadium. We soon learned that the sunny side soon became the shady side.

After the Bull Fights we would usually go to the Florida Club for dinner. This was a white tablecloth restaurant where a steak dinner was $1.50 and a mixed drink was $.20. Of course our monthly pay was less than $90.00.

Our training ended in the middle of December and we were released at that time to go home. We were given a travel allowance of about $95.00. A number of the trainees chartered a bus to try to save some of those funds but it was going to be a three day ride.

Ralph and I decided to fly. Our flight went from El Paso to Dallas to Washington and cost us $95.00

I arrived back in Washington just before Christmas. I went back to Pennsylvania to spend the Christmas holidays. After Christmas I returned to the Washington DC area and started job hunting. Before I left for active duty in the Army, I had taken the government test for the Federal Register, a requirement to obtain a job in the government sector. Before leaving for basic training I was offered a job in the Government Services Administration. However, since I was going on active duty, I had to decline the offer. I requested that I be given a six month leave of absence until I returned. This was granted.

When I returned I reconnected with Bob, my prior roommate and found that he was now living in a two bedroom basement apartment in McLean. He was looking for a roommate. We agreed to share the apartment.

I also applied to American University to continue my education and I was accepted into their Business Program. I decided to continue by going to night school two nights a week. I took two classes a semester and one in the summer.

Now I needed a job .I went to American Security & Trust to see if there were any job opportunities available that I might qualify for. I was offered a position as a junior investment analyst in their Investment Department at a salary of $3,850 a year. Again, one of the benefits was a "free checking account."

I also stopped at the branch where I had been a teller. Mike was there, the man who ran the numbers in Washington. He asked me what I was going to do and I told him I was looking for a job. He said that I should come and work for him. He offered me $10,000, twice what I would eventually receive. In 2016 dollars this was over $79,000. I thought about it for about 15 seconds, thanked him but I said that I did not want to come home after work every day looking over my shoulder. He said he understood but that the job was there if I changed my mind.

Chapter Three
Department of Commerce

I activated my job search in the government sector and received an offer for an accounting intern position in the Office of the Secretary of Commerce. This office was responsible for the accounting functions of the Secretary of Commerce and paid $4,350 per year, which was $34,700 in 2016 dollars.

I decided to take this job. John F. Kennedy had just been elected President of the United States and had appointed Luther Hodges, the former Governor of North Carolina, to be the Secretary of Commerce. The accounting office for the Office of the Secretary also included the International Trade Fairs Department. An organization that promoted U.S. Business throughout the world by putting on trade fairs and having U.S. Industry demonstrate their products. This was an attempt to increase exports.

The accounting function was housed in the Old Saint Elizabeth Hospital Building off of Pennsylvania Ave. near the Capitol.

As an accounting intern I was to be assigned to the different accounting departments – accounts payable, budgeting, and payroll. I was to learn the operation from the bottom up.

I was first assigned to the accounts payable or voucher department. I was then sent to the payroll department and finally the budgeting department.

The accounts payable department was responsible for preparing invoices and sending them to the Treasury Department for payment. There were two employees in this department and I made three. You took the invoices and compared them to the documentation and if everything was in order you put an appropriation number on them and sent them to the Treasury Department for payment. When they came back from the Treasury Department you filed the documentation. This was not difficult but there was a significant backlog.

I was taught the process and then given a stack of vouchers to process. The two accounts payable employees were processing about 25 vouchers each per day. After I became competent with the process I was easily doing over 50 vouchers a day. In a few weeks there were no more backlogs and I was transferred to the payroll department.

After about 30 days I was transferred back to accounts payable, as the backlog had grown. In a short period of time the backlog was gone and I was transferred back to the budget department.

After a month or so I was transferred back to accounts payable as the backlog had grown again. It was obvious that the other employees were never going to do more than about 25 vouchers a day.

Shortly after I started working at the Department of Commerce I met my future wife. The phone that my roommate and I shared had been the previous tenant's number. If we hadn't accepted that number it would have been months before we received phone service. One Sunday evening the phone rang looking for the girls that had previously rented the apartment. I answered and proceeded to talk with the young woman on the other end, Amy. I invited my roommate and I over to their apartment for a cup of coffee. We went to their apartment in Rosslyn, VA. One of Amy's roommates would become my future wife. Sharon Mead was working for the C.I.A. in the temporary quarters by the reflecting pool in Washington, D.C., The Langley, VA. facility was under construction but had not been completed. In 1960 there were World War II temporary wooden office buildings lining the reflecting pool and also on Constitution Ave.

Sharon didn't appear to be interested in me but after a number of calls she finally agreed to go out with me. I would stop by after school in the evening and we would go to a Marriott's "Hot Shoppes" for something to eat. The Hot Shoppes was a drive-in style restaurant where you could order from your car via a radio type device and food would be delivered and a tray anchored to your window. After a few months we became a couple and in May 1961 we became engaged and set October 7th as the date to be married.

Sharon was from Fort Madison, Iowa and had been recruited by the C.I.A. from a Business School in Minneapolis, MN to work for the C.I.A. in Washington, D.C. Fort Madison was similar to Clearfield, a blue collar and agricultural oriented town. Their claim to fame was that the Sheaffer Pen Company was headquartered there. Both of Sharon's parents, Vincil & Lorraine Mead, worked there for many years. Her father served in the U.S. Army during World War II and participated in the African and Italian Campaigns. Sharon was the first to permanently leave the area.

We were married on Saturday, October 7th in the Catholic Church in McLean, VA. It was family and close friends only. We had a small wedding lunch at the Evan's Farm Inn in McLean where my Best Man, Herb Hudson, was also the night manager. Herb was also a co-worker at the Commerce Department.

The week before I was scheduled to be married, October 7, 1961, the Director called me into his office and advised me that I needed to slow down. He said I was working too fast and that I needed to slow down because I might make mistakes. I asked him if I had made any mistakes and he said no but that I might. He also said that I was working myself out of a job. If I continued he might have to make some personnel reductions. Since I was the last to be hired I would be the first to be fired. He also said that he was a Grade 13 government employee and that his grade was dependent upon the number of people that he had working for him. He was not going to jeopardize that.

I told him that I understood. Obviously this bothered me but since I was going to be married in a week I decided to forget about it for the time being.

We had planned to spend our honeymoon on the "Outer Banks" of North Carolina.

We got lost Saturday evening and found a motel in the middle of peanut country outside of Richmond to spend the night. The restaurant attached to the motel had two entrances. One said "Whites" only and the other said "Colored." Having grown up in Central Pennsylvania I had never seen or experienced segregation. This was a shock. I realized we were now in the South and things were different. We were happy to get on the road in the morning.

After a few days on the Outer Banks, my last conversation with the Director at the Commerce Department began to bother me. So much so that I said to my new wife that we needed to cut short our honeymoon and go back so I could start to look for a new job. What a way to start a new life! Fortunately, Sharon was a trooper and said ok. On Wednesday morning we returned home and I went to the job office at Benjamin Franklin University to see what opportunities might exist.

I was told that a C.P.A. firm, Main & Company, was looking for Junior Accountants. I asked how I would proceed and the placement officer said that she would call and set up an appointment. Although I wasn't exactly sure what a C.P.A. firm did, I though why not? She arraigned for me to meet the General Partner, Howard Malloy, the next morning.

Jess & Sharon - Wedding Oct. 7, 1961

Sharon's Parents -Vincil & Loraine Mead , Jess & Sharon,
Elizabeth & Elmer Sweely

Sharon & Parents

Chapter Four
Main & Co.

Main & Co. was located at 13th and Pennsylvania in the Pennsylvania Building. I went there after lunch on Thursday and met Howard Malloy, the General Partner. He asked various questions about me, my background and experience and then I met the resident partner, Charles (Chuck) Haas. I learned that this office of Main & Company was opened a few years before. The main office was in Pittsburgh, Pa. They were considered one of the leading union auditors in the nation. They also had a number of additional offices around the country.

They had opened the Washington office to handle the AFL-CIO Union audit and were growing their business from there.

Main & Company considered themselves one of the Big 10 Accounting Firms in the U.S. (This meant nothing to me).

They asked me why I wanted to leave my current job and I explained what had occurred.

I felt that I interacted well with both the General and Resident partners. They told me that they would be in touch and I thanked them for the opportunity to meet with them.

The following day, Friday, I received a call from Chuck Haas and was offered a position as a junior accountant at the starting rate of $4,500 a year, which was $35,900 in 2016 dollars. Vacation of one week a year and health insurance for the family was included. In those days this was not expensive. I believe that my cost for healthcare was about $2.00 a week.

I thanked him for the offer and asked if I could have until Monday to give them an answer. Chuck said that would be fine. I spent the week-end discussing the pros and cons with Sharon. She agreed that whatever I wanted to do, she would be behind me. I knew that I could not continue, with not working to my full capacity, at the Commerce Department, On Monday I called Chuck and told him that I would like to accept the junior accountant's position.

I needed to give my current employer two weeks' notice. He agreed that was acceptable, so my next step was to go to my boss and advise him that I would be leaving in two weeks. After doing that I felt as though the weight of the world had been lifted off my shoulders. He wasn't happy but I knew that I had made the right decision.

My next step was to tell my Uncle Fred what I was going to do. He said that if I felt this was the right thing to do then do it. My parents however weren't as accepting. They had lived through the "Great Depression" and my father had only one job his entire life. He spent over 45 years as a master mechanic on the New York Central Railroad. They thought I had gone off the deep end. I told them to trust me and that everything would be ok.

I reported to my new employer two weeks later, October 30, 1961. I was introduced to everyone and given an orientation as to what would be expected of me.

There were a total of 6 employees in the Washington office.

At Main & Co. we would be working a minimum of 5 days a week in the off season and during the "busy" season (November through April) we could be working at least 6 days a week. The job was a salary position and we were paid once a month.

Main and Co. only did attestation work and no "write up" work. This was all new to me but I quickly learned the difference. We also did tax returns for our clients and their executives. We did not do tax returns on a walk in basis.

Our clients included labor unions, non-profit organizations, banks & financial institutions, manufacturing companies (some public and some private), real estate developers, education associations, mortgage brokers and apartment cooperatives among others.

The job of a junior accountant was to do whatever the partner in charge wanted you to do. I learned to reconcile bank accounts, run a 10 key adding machine with a tape, set up work papers and analyze general ledger accounts. I learned how the balance sheet and the profit and loss statement interacted and if an error was divisible by 9 it was probably a transposition. The real world compared to "book learning."

It was expected that you would take the CPA exam as soon as you were eligible to take it. If you didn't pass the first time, it was expected that you would pass at least two parts and then pass the remaining parts within two years. If you weren't successful doing that then the firm would try to place you with one of their clients. This was good for both the individual as well as the client.

We had no women working as accountants at the firm and in the 1960's there weren't that many women with the large firms. One of our General Partners close business friend ran the CADES Coaching Course for the CPA Exam in Washington, D.C. He had a daughter who had recently graduated from college with a degree in accounting. She became the first woman hired in our office. She was extremely bright and she fit in well. There was no problem in the office but our clients would not accept her. The clients put pressure on our General Partner to not send her on their audits. This was sad and within the first year she moved on. The General Partner needed to keep our clients satisfied.

One of the most important aspects of the job was to set up your work papers for whatever the task was…problem solving. By setting up your work papers, the task of analyzing different accounts was made simpler. This would hold true in later life in problem solving and reaching decisions. We used 7 column, 14 column and 21 column workpaper. Today the laptop computer, with Excell has replaced that.

We would be interacting with different people at the clients and we would be working mostly at their location except when we were finalizing the audit report in the office. We were told that we were not to be confrontational and if we had questions see the person in charge of the audit. We also did special jobs for clients such as internal control analysis and systems reviews.

We were also told that "fraternization" with the employees of our clients was unacceptable. Dating employees was unacceptable. This could possibly compromise our independence. I don't know if that is still the norm today.

In the early 1960's most of our clients used either an NCR Accounting Machine or a Remington Rand Accounting Machine. Some were using punch card systems such as IBM's accounting machine. Large scale computers such as an IBM 1401 were just coming on line.

We had portable 10 key adding machines with tapes. These were used to foot ledgers and check balances.

Then, as today, the question in doing an audit is whether to audit "through" or "around" the computer. I am not sure that there is still a clear answer.

I had taken all of the accounting courses and tax courses in school. I had intermediate and advanced accounting, fund accounting, auditing, cost accounting, tax accounting but nothing prepared me for my job in a public accounting firm.

In the 1960's there were public accounting firms and public accounting firms. In order to sit for the C.P.A. exam in the District of Columbia you were required to have two years of public accounting experience. This could not be just any public accounting experience. It had to be with a firm that did attestation work and not "write up" work. In fact, even though the C.P.A. exam was uniform, some states required an additional section, i.e. Maryland – Economics. Most states required at least two years of experience before you were eligible to even sit for the exam. In Virginia, you could sit for the exam but you would not be granted a license until you had two years' experience.

Obviously things have changed today. Even though the exam is still uniform, most states now require 150 college credits before you can sit. The experience requirement appears easier today because of the reliance on the 150 credits. I am not sure that I agree but then I am "old school."

Today there are still 4 parts to the Uniform exam but they are mostly multiple choice. Also no experience is required to sit for the exam. You need 150 credits and a college degree from a four year school. No public accounting experience is required. It appears that it is much more an academic exam.

In the past, the exam was only given twice a year but today it is given at least 8 times. Also, in the past you were required to take the entire exam and you needed to pass at least two parts in order to retain them going forward. If you didn't past the remaining parts in a certain number of sittings, you had to start over.

Today you can take one part at a time and it isn't necessary to pass it to take another part. If you take one part at a time and pass the four parts then some consider that you have passed the exam the first time. Not in the past. Then you had to take and pass all four parts the first time to have "passed the exam the first time."

We were not allowed to bring an abacus or any type of adding machine to the exam. Only a pencil. All adding, etc. had to be done in your head or on paper. Battery operated adding machines did not exist in the early 1960's. Your calculations for the problems in the practice section had to be shown in detail.

I do think that the professional designation, C.P.A. has been watered down today because of the changes that have occurred even though the pass rates are similar.

Today there is much more compartmentalization then there was 60 years ago. We not only did the audit we also did the tax returns and any management information studies. This gave us a more well-rounded view of the client as we were involved in all aspects of the operation.

In the 1960's we also had a dress code. We had to wear business suits with white shirts, regular ties, a hat and overcoat. No gaudy jewelry. In the summer we had to wear a straw hat and in the winter a felt had. This was similar to what IBM required of their salesforce. We had to exhibit a professional look. The book "Dress for Success" was never more accurate.

We were also not allowed to fraternize or date any employees of our clients. This was so there would be no question of our independence. If we were caught dating we were subject to dismissal. Independence and ethical behavior was stressed over and over.

If we were having a business lunch with a client and the client had a drink, we were allowed to also have a drink but we were not to go back to the client's office. We were to return to the office for the balance of the day. Basic rules but with a definite value to all of them.

The staffing when I joined the Washington office of Main & Co. consisted of a General Partner, two resident partners, a senior accountant and two junior accountants. This group was supported by an administrative assistant who was responsible for typing the reports using a typewriter. Over the years we expanded the lower ranks of the firm, junior accountants and semi-senior accountants and everyone did a little more each year. There were no personal computers or laptops in those days. There were no electronic calculators either. Slide rules were a fall back.

I am not sure how the billing rates were established but my billing rate was initially $15 per hour and we were expected to bill at least 2,500 hours per year. This would mean annual billings of $37,500 and my annual salary was $4,500 or approximately an 8.3 to 1 ratio. As I moved up the rank from a junior accountant to a semi-senior to a senior my annual compensation grew to where I was making $9,500 annually in 1966 which was $69,900 in 2016 dollars.

At the same time a resident partner was making about $12,500 which was $92,000 in 2016 dollars. The resident partners shared in the profits of the local office while the General Partner shared in the profits of the firm as a whole.

The lower ranking employees were also paid overtime. The more you worked the less you earned per hour. As an example, the base hours for a month was 160. If you worked 200 hours, you divided the monthly rate of $375 per month by 200 hours, overtime would be paid at $1.875 per hour or 40 overtime hours at $1.875. If you worked 250 hours then overtime hours would be paid at $1.50 per hour. The more you worked the less you were paid per hour for the overtime hours.

I don't know who designed this process but this was standard throughout Main & Company.

It was expected that you knew how to play golf as you moved up the ranks in the firm. The higher you progressed the more probability there was that golf became important. A lot of business was transacted on the golf course.

I had never played golf. I am a natural left hander and in high school I tried to join the golf club but I broke the golf machine and was asked to please leave.

There was a golf course in Annandale, Virginia called Pinecrest. The resident partner suggested that we play one Saturday morning and obviously I said ok. You could rent clubs there. I met Chuck and off we went. I knew that most golfing folks talked about breaking 100. When we finished our round, I had shoot 110. I thought wow! I didn't think this was such a hard game after all! That was until I found out that it was a par 3 course, for a total par of 54. Then I realized that 110 wasn't very good after all.

Fortunately one of our hires in 1962 was a young man who had graduated from the University of Maryland and was on their golf team. Ron was a scratch golfer. From that time on until I left the firm Ron and I played at least once a week. Of course, I received some one on one coaching and my game improved.

In 1961, when John F. Kennedy was in the White House, it was publicized that President Kennedy was learning to speed read to keep up with all his reading by taking a course in speed reading from VICORE (Visual Conception Reading). Our General Partner was considering going back to college and working toward a Master's and maybe a Doctorate. He thought he would like to teach when he retired from Public Accounting. Because of his age he was self-conscious and decided that he needed an edge and maybe speed reading was the answer. One morning he called a meeting of all of the employees, we were now up to about 10, and announced that we were all going to be required to take the speed reading course. The firm would pay for it and we would come in to the office early, two days a week, before we went to a client. The course would last for 10 to 12 weeks.

No one was happy because it was a "command performance." However, this was one of the most valuable programs I have ever participated in. The techniques that were taught have lasted me my entire career. I still use them today and it was particularly beneficial as I finished my education at American University and later my Master's at George Washington University.

You learned to read down instead of across. You also learned to read at different speeds, depending on what the subject matter was. You learned to read faster with greater comprehension. I can read a newspaper at over 5,000 words per minute and a novel at close to the same with over 90% comprehension. It does no good to read fast if you don't comprehend what you have read.

You also learned that you might read word by word for certain matter, i.e. technical journals, etc. Your speed is dependent on the subject matter.

I am forever thankful that I was required to attend these sessions. It was well worth the effort. I still wonder today why this isn't taught in high school or first year college.

In 1963 and 1964, I was starting to be responsible for some of the firm's smaller jobs. The AICPA had also come out with a standard test for firms to use in the selection process of new accountants. It was very academic and tested text book knowledge. Our General Partner decided that he was going to use it to screen potential new hires. One of the first was a young man who had just graduated from college. He scored off the charts, in the 95th percentile.

He was hired and he was assigned to work with me on one or two jobs. I was concerned because his social skills were lacking. He appeared to be very bright but unable to communicate well.

We were getting ready to do the advance audit work up on an excavating client that was headquartered across from Fort McNair in South West, D.C. I was assigned to start the audit and this young man was assigned to work for me. We usually used the cafeteria at Fort McNair to have lunch. The buildings were World War II vintage. We could walk down a long hallway to the cafeteria or down the outside of the building and enter at the cafeteria entrance.

One day it was raining and we decided to walk inside. As we were walking down the hallway there were "WET PAINT" signs all over. The inside of the building was being painted. At a junction in the hall there were a number of phone booths and they had been painted and wet paint signs were posted all over the front. John stopped and looked at the phone booths and then went into one, closed the door and made a phone call. In a few minutes he exited and his suit had wet paint all over it from the phone booth. I said to him, "didn't you see that they had just painted the phone booths" and he answered, "yes, but I had to make a phone call."

In a few weeks John was no longer with us and the AICPA test was no longer used.

I planned to take the C.P.A. exam in November 1964 in Washington, DC. It was recommended that you should take a preparatory course. I decided to take the CADES CPA Coaching course that was taught by Seymour Kaufman. Seymour also taught at Benjamin Franklin University and American University. This was considered the best course in the Washington area and had the highest pass ratio. It was a 6 month program, three nights a week for 4 hours a night and four hours Saturday mornings. Saturday mornings were simulated examinations. This resulted in 20 hours a week in class and another 20 hours a week studying and at least 40 to 50 hours a week working.

I was still going to American University night school. I decided to take the summer and the fall semester off to study for the C.P.A. exam. I asked for and received a "leave of absence" from American.

When I started the CADES program, Seymour told us that when we went home we needed to tell our spouse or significant other that for the next six months don't expect to see much of us. She or he would have to cut the grass, deal with the children and do all of the household chores. He was right. It took that kind of dedication to make it through the program successful. However, passing the first time would make it all worthwhile.

At this time we had two children, Robin age 3 and Scott, age 2. Sharon would have to deal with the house and them for the next 6 months with little help from me.

I took the C.P.A. exam in November 1964 in the "Old National Guard Armory" in Washington, D.C. It was a grueling three days. On Friday, after finishing the exam, I felt like I had just gone 10 rounds with Joe Louis. I went home and slept most of the week-end.

In February, I was on a job with the resident-partner, Chuck Haas, when he received a call from the office. He told me that my wife had called and I needed to call her. This was unusual because we never received phone calls from home unless it was an emergency. I called home and Sharon said that there was an envelope in the mail from the DC Board of Accountancy. I told her to open it and tell me what it was. She did and she yelled, "You passed."

I was in shock and said, "Great, see you tonight."

Chuck asked me if everything was ok and I said, "I passed."

He said we have to celebrate. We stopped work and went to an early lunch, along with a few other staff members, and had a few drinks. What a relief!

I was fortunate in that I passed all four parts the first time. I would not have wanted to do it again. All the time and effort for the past six months was worth it.

Sharon and I stayed in our first apartment for a little over a year. She continued working at the C.I.A. and rode the bus from the bottom of the hill from our apartment to Langley. Langley had just opened. A few months after we were married Sharon announced that she was pregnant.

A surprise to all. In June of 1961, Robin was born in Alexandria, VA. Sharon quit a few months before the birth and we were now a one salary family. Sharon decided to stay home and raise our baby.

We decided that we needed more room so we began looking for a small home. My salary at the time was $6,000 a year. We found that the only thing that would fit our budget was in Woodbridge, VA. where Hylton Enterprises was developing new homes that were affordable. We started to look because our lease was up in September of 1961. We were paying $95.00 a month for our apartment. We found a new home model that we liked and it was $14,000. We would be able to borrow most of the funds on an FHA loan and our monthly payment would be $95.00 a month.

The model we choose was two levels, three bedrooms and 2 baths. I think that the total square footage was only a little over 1,000 but it suited us. We would be 26 miles from downtown Washington but not a bad commute. I think we moved in late 1962.

As I look back, we were newly married, I had a new job and was going to school two nights a week and Sharon was home with our first child and didn't drive. I give her all the credit in the world for the glue that held us together. She deserves all the credit for my ability to grow and move forward.

I was promoted to Semi-senior accountant after passing the exam. In the 1960's Northern Virginia was mostly the home of government employees while The Maryland suburbs of the District of Columbia was the home to the business community. Our second child, Scott was born in November of 1963 while we were still living in Woodbridge. He was also born in Alexandria.

I was continuing to advance at work and we decided that our next step was to try to find a home in the Maryland suburbs. In early 1964 we started to look at possible areas. We found a new development in Rockville, MD (only 15 miles from our D.C. office) and a home that should suit us for quite a while. The home we selected was about $22,000 but was at least twice as large as our Woodbridge home and came with a number of amenities, including all gas, a carport and a family room as well as a living room and dining room. It was two stories and had 4 bedrooms and 2 ½ baths and a full unfinished basement and two fireplaces.

We decided to buy and a few months later we moved after selling our first home. Our monthly payment was now $200.00 a month with a traditional loan with 10% down.

After passing the C.P.A. exam, I went in to see my advisor at American University and told her that I had passed the C.P.A. exam and asked if I could get any credit toward my degree. She said she would see what could be done. I received a letter soon thereafter advising me that I didn't need to take any additional accounting courses but that I still had to take some courses. As a compromise I took 30 credits of graduate level business courses. As a result, when I did enroll for an M.B.A., I only needed 30 hours of credits instead of 60.

The following are excerpts from some of the experiences that I was exposed to in my Public Accounting Career. I hope that you find them as interesting today as they were to me some 60 years ago.

Chapter Five
My First Assignment as a Junior Accountant:

One of the first jobs that I went on at Main & Co. was the National Labor Union, The AFL-CIO.

I was directed to do the menial tasks such as account analysis, bank reconciliations, etc. One of the accountants for the AFL-CIO was assigned to assist us in finding anything that we might need help with.

The AFL-CIO had a Remington-Rand computer system and also Remington-Rand typewriters. At the time, IBM was considered the best computer system available and also IBM had the best typewriters. I had taken a number of basic computer courses at American University and had a decent understanding of how they worked and what was available.

The employees at the AFL-CIO were constantly complaining about the computer system breaking down and the typewriters not working efficiently.

At lunch one day, I said to our contact that they should consider looking at IBM equipment as it was considered the "Gold Standard." I wasn't aware at the time that IBM was non-union while Remington-Rand was unionized.

The following day, Howard Malloy, the General Partner, appeared on site and asked me to come with him. We went into an empty office and he proceeded to tell me that I needed to be more aware of what I said and who I said it to. He said that The Controller of the AFL-CIO had called him last evening and complained about me talking about IBM with his employee. The AFL-CIO was a major client and I needed to be more sensitive when dealing with their employees. I received a royal chewing out and told that if this happened again I would be removed from the job and maybe I wouldn't have a job.

My Father had been a member of a union his whole career. This was a wakeup call for me as it never crossed my mind that the level of union versus non-union was so sensitive. Another step in my education in the world of business. I never made that mistake again. However, it certainly changed my views of union versus non-union.

The AFL-CIO had a department called COPE (Committee on Political Education) in its organization. The purpose of this organization was to education all of its union members during an election as to where those running for election stood on the issues. A portion of the union members' dues went into this organization. A union cannot tell its members how to vote but they can "educate" them.

This was accomplished by taking a sheet of paper and putting the individual running for office on it and then putting pro or con and listing the issues under pro or con. In effect, telling them who to vote for.

In the 1960's the Washington Gas Light Company and the AFL-CIO's office employees were unionized in the same local union. Union negotiations were on going with the International and the local but they weren't going well. The local decided that they would go on strike and put up a strike wall at both office locations. George Meany was the AFL-CIO's President then and when he heard of this he told the negotiators for the International to settle it now. The last thing they needed was a strike in front of their headquarters. No strike ever materialized.

Chapter Six
A Union Embezzlement

When I was still a junior accountant I was assigned to work on the audit of the International Union of Electrical Radio and Machine Workers, a labor union. Main & Co. had been doing the audit of this union for a number of years and the audit program had not changed significantly over that period of time.

The union had a number of organizers in the field whose job was to try to organize non-union shops in their districts. In addition to their salary, they were also reimbursed for travel and other expenses incurred, including gasoline for their automobiles.

The union had gasoline credit cards with two different oil companies. Monthly, the oil companies would submit a box of gasoline purchases on gasoline credit cards that the individual had signed at the gas station. These boxes contained computer cards that were already sorted by individual and by date of purchase.

The union would then reimburse the oil company. My job was to analyze these cards to see if the total matched the check that had been sent to the oil company. I decided to also take a look at the cards to see if the amount of purchase was reasonable.

Since these cards were arranged by individual and date, it was fairly straight forward to review. I selected a month and ran a calculator tape on the cards to see if they agreed to the total. In the early days of computers we were auditing "around the computer." When I started to review a number of the individual transactions I found a number of discrepancies. A number of the individuals were purchasing an incredible number of gallons of gasoline within a few days. It was impossible that they could have driven that much in that amount of time. Also, I found that the purchase of gas on a number of occasions was over a thousand miles apart on the same day, again an impossible situation.

I discussed this with the partner on the job and he indicated that I should compare where they were purchasing gas with their expense reports. I selected a few individuals to do this with and found that where they said they were per their expense reports didn't agree with where they were purchasing gasoline. I brought this to the attention of the partner and it was decided that we needed to expand our audit review.

We began to look at those individuals where we found serious discrepancies and saw that there was a pattern with those that were supposed to be organizing in Erie, Pa. In reviewing their expense reports in depth, I noticed that they were all staying at the Dearborn Manor Motel. Receipts for the motel were from a receipt book that you could buy from any office supply company and they were stamped with Dearborn Manor Motel.

Main & Co. had just purchased a CPA firm in Erie, Pa. so the partner contacted a partner in Erie and asked them to check out this motel. We received a phone call that said that there was no Dearborn Manor Motel and that the address was a fishing shack along Lake Erie. They followed up with a rental company and found that this shack had been rented to one of the organizers on a long term basis.

We knew that we had uncovered a serious problem but we didn't know how big the problem was. The organizers were padding their expense reports with false receipts and they were in collusion with some of the gasoline station operators. We found that they would get kick-backs from the gasoline station operators for false receipts.

The General Partner met with the Executive Director of the Union to discuss our findings and where did they want us to go. The issue was so pervasive that we had no idea how large the problem was and how long it had been going on. The Union was advised that we would not be able to render an unqualified opinion on their financial statements because of these discrepancies. A labor union also had to file a financial report with The U.S. Department of Labor under the Langrum-Griffin Act.

The Executive Director of the Union was not happy with our firm and fired us from the audit job. They hired a local CPA firm who gave them an unqualified opinion and filed the Labor Department reports.

The FBI became involved and wanted to indict many of the organizers but somewhere it was sweep under the rug during the early days of the JFK Presidency.

No one within their organization was fired and no one was prosecuted. Our audit fee for the job was $10,000. But Main & Company was ethical and decided it wasn't worth doing something that they could not defend.

— ⦿ —

Chapter Seven
Embezzlement on a Grand Scale:

In the early 1960's, Main & Company merged with F.W. LaFrentz & Co. to become Main LaFrentz. In many cities there were offices for both companies and therefore an integration of the business had to happen. In Washington, D.C. both firms had offices and the decision was made by the General Partner of Main & Co. for the personnel of Main & Co. to head up the audits of the major F.W. LaFrentz clients.

One of F.W. Lafrentz's clients was "The American Chemical Society." The American Chemical Society (ACS) was the non-profit trade association for those in the chemical world. The ACS had its main headquarters in Washington, D.C. and their Abstract Services Operation in Columbus, OH. The ACS was the recipient of a number of grants for specific projects. As a result they utilized Fund Accounting for these programs (a self-balancing chart of accounts). These Funds were incorporated into the overall financial statements for the society.

Normally, we would start a preliminary analysis of the audit during the third quarter of the year and then come back after the books were closed at the beginning of the New Year to complete the examination. Since this was a new account to us, we had to understand the client's business and determine the approach that the audit would take.

I was a senior on the job and was assigned the task of reviewing a number of the funds. One of the funds was "The Petroleum Research Fund." This Fund was substantial in nature and had been initially funded by companies in the Petroleum industry. These funds were invested in various bonds, stocks and mutual funds. The interest earned was substantial. The purpose of this Fund was to fund research projects in the Petroleum arena.

One of the major functions of the ACS was to educate members of the ACS by providing meetings/seminars throughout the year at various locations throughout the United States. Generally there were two or more each year with over 1,000 in attendance at each meeting. There was a fee paid by the attendee that could amount to $500 or more. In addition, many of the publications of the ACS were sold at these meetings. Some registered in advance and sent their money in to the main headquarters but many waited and registered and paid at the meeting. Cash payments were significant at these meetings .To handle the money that was paid at the meetings, an account was established at a local bank to deposit these funds. Deposits were made throughout the meetings and then a check was issued once the meeting was over and deposited into a bank account at headquarters and a reconciliation made to account for all the monies.

As I began my analysis of the Petroleum Research Fund, I made a calculation of the interest that was earned on the assets and found that there was a significant difference between what the interest should have been and what was recorded in the books. In addition there were numerous journal entries reducing the Fund Balance with the explanation that it was to correct erroneous transactions that were credited to the wrong fund. This appeared unusual and I brought this up to the

Resident Partner on the job. He had been looking at some of the other transactions recorded in the books and said that he had the other side of the entry. This meant that he had the credit and it was in the meetings/seminars account.

He told me that I needed to determine when and where the erroneous deposit had been made and determine that the correcting journal entry was correct. The journal entry did not include any detail concerning that so I made a list of the entries and went to the Controller of the ACS and asked him to assist me in determining information concerning the erroneous deposits. The Controller indicated that he was tied up but that he would get that information for me the next day.

The following day the Managing/General Partner of Main LaFrentz, Howard Malloy, came to the job site to meet with the resident partner and advise him that the Controller had gone to the President of ACS and advised him that he had been embezzling money from the ACS and that the auditors had caught up to him.

As a result we were to modify our audit program and look into this in greater depth to determine the magnitude of the embezzlement.

What we found was that the embezzlement of funds by the Controller had been going on for at least five years and had amounted to over $5 million. The embezzlement was quite sophisticated. One of the other Funds that he was using was with the National Science Foundation (NSF). The Controller handled the funding requests himself from the NSF. Whenever there was a meeting scheduled, the Controller would request additional funding from the NSF. When the check arrived from the

NFS he would not deposit it but take it with him to the meeting.

Since significant cash was generated at these meetings, he would make the deposits himself at the local bank. He would take cash from the meetings and replace it with the check from the NSF so that the receipts would balance. He would place the cash in his briefcase and hand carry it back to Washington on an airplane. He later indicated that sometimes he would put the cash in his luggage and check it on the airplane. When asked "wasn't he concerned it might get lost," his comment was "while I didn't have it when I went." When he arrived back in Washington he would place it in the equivalent of a safe deposit box that was in a walk in bank type safe in the accounting department. He would leave it in that safe deposit box until he invested it. He indicated that at different times he was in the elevator with the President of the ACS and he had $10,000 or more in his briefcase that he was taking home.

In order to get the funds in the NSF to balance, he would make a journal entry to credit the Petroleum Research Fund, reducing the Fund, and debiting the National Science Foundation Fund (increasing it for the check that he had deposited at the meeting). He said that he knew that the auditors never reconciled the funds in the Petroleum Research Fund so he used that Fund to hide his embezzlement.

He had been successful in doing this for at least 5 years and he planned to stop but then he thought that he would do it one more time. In this case it was once too many.

He had invested the embezzlement funds in the stock market at the time that the market had been going up. He paid back everything that we were able to identify that had been embezzled. The ACS chose not to file charges against him because of the publicity but terminated his services. It was believed that he had made much more from investing these funds then he paid back but that was never determined.

A year later, he asked the Managing/General Partner of the accounting firm Main LaFrentz, for a reference for an accounting position at another employer.

Chapter Eight
Political Action Committee

One of our clients was the Association of American Colleges. Included in that organization was something called the "Political Action Committee" headed by Richard Scanlon. Scanlon was one of the first to analyze and predict election results based upon prior results and the correlation with various factors. He was also one of the first to use computers. His models were so good that he was eventually hired as a consultant to the news networks during elections. He was later made Director of the United States Census.

These were the type of individuals that we met during audits and the exposure was something that no other field could give you.

Chapter Nine
American Security & Trust – Pension Fund

One of the audits that we did was the American Security & Trust Pension Plan. American Security had their own employee pension plan and had documents that they were required to file annually. The major work was to determine if the calculations of their pensions were being done correctly. Having worked at American Security, prior to Main & Company, I was assigned to work with the resident partner on this job. The interesting fact is that I knew some of the individuals that were being reviewed. I hadn't realized, when I worked there as a teller, that bank salaries were not high. The prestige of working at a bank along with free checking and lower interest rates on loans was what the bank was selling to their employees.

One of the individuals that we had decided to test was the Sr. VP of the Investment Department. He was retiring after spending over 40 years at the bank. His salary upon retiring was $9,500. I thought how lucky I was that I decided not to return to the bank. You can't eat "prestige."

Chapter Ten
Inventory – WESCO/WASCO

One of the clients of our Pittsburgh home office was Westinghouse Electric. Westinghouse had a number of divisions. WESCO was the Westinghouse Electric Supply Company and included small counter type electrical home appliances. WASCO was the Westinghouse Appliance Supply Company and included large items like washers, dryers, refrigerators, etc. They also owned a number of radio and television stations.

Although we weren't involved in the audit, the Washington DC office was asked to observe inventory taking and doing some test counts at the Richmond, VA. warehouse.

I was sent to Richmond, VA. in 1961 to observe the year end taking of the WASCO inventory at their Richmond warehouse. I was given a number of punch cards with certain descriptions of items and my job was to observe the inventory taking and count the items that I had punch cards for.

This was a typical job for a junior accountant. I was sent to Richmond and had to stay overnight. Having never done this before, I had some trepidation but figured that it couldn't be too difficult. In 1961 Richmond was a segregated city and not very progressive. The warehouse was on a wharf in the James River.

I met the WASCO folks who were going to do the inventory and I observed the inventory taking. I also took the punch cards and did my independent inventory counts. The appliances were in cardboard boxes and I had no idea if what was marked on the boxes was correct, I also found some boxes that were empty and mentioned this to the head of the WASCO inventory. No one seemed to know why they were empty.

Upon completion of observing the inventory I wrote up a brief summary and took my punch cards and gave them to one of the resident partners. I never heard anything further so I assumed all was well.

Chapter Eleven
Inventory – Potomac Sand & Gravel

Another client was the Potomac Sand & Gravel Company. They were located under the Whitehurst Freeway in Georgetown, along the Potomac River. They provided sand and gravel to most of the concrete companies in the Washington area. They would ship sand and gravel from their quarries in Southern Maryland on barges, up the Potomac River, and off load them at their Georgetown facility. Some of the gravel went into silos and others were in piles on the ground. The same was true for the sand. There were different types of sand as well as gravel.

At the end of each year we had to observe inventory and do test counts of the different types of sand and gravel. One of the employees of Potomac Sand & Gravel was assigned to work with us to identify the type of gravel or sand that we were inventorying.

There were ropes with knots tied in them at each silo. To take the inventory we would climb to the top of the silo and throw the rope in and count the number of knots. We then took a conversion table that calculated the number of tons per knot. For the piles of sand and gravel that were on the ground, their employee would tell us the type of sand or gravel and they would estimate how many tons were in the pile.

We took their word and didn't try to independently verify they type or tonnage. You can estimate the tonnage by using a mathematical formula using circumference and height but I was told that we should just use their estimate.

We also didn't verify the type of gravel in the silos or the calculation of the knots.

I was always somewhat concerned because this was during the time of the "Billy Sol Estes" scandal and the American Crude Vegetable Oil "Salad Oil" scandal.

In the salad oil scandal case, management had used their inventory for bank loans but the ships that had arrived at docks weren't full of salad oil. The ships were mostly full of water with just a little salad oil on top. Over $150 million dollars in 1963 was lost ($1.1 billion in 2008 dollars).

Chapter Twelve
Personal tax Return- Trading in Commodities

We did not do walk in tax returns but we would do tax returns for executives of the firms we audited.

I was given the tax return of an executive with a non-profit to prepare. As I took all of his information and started to organize it I realized that he was a huge commodity trader. I was used to stock trades but I had never encountered a commodity trader. As I organized his trades I knew that I needed to do some homework in commodity trading.

This individual had traded every type of commodity you could think of. Pork Bellies, cattle, cotton, corn soybeans, etc. Each different commodity trade involves a different standard of measurement. The total trades totaled over $750,000 on which he had lost money in the aggregate. I knew that some people had made huge returns in commodities but the risk profile was extremely high. This was such a situation. In the following years this individual returned to stock and bond trading and left commodities alone.

Chapter Thirteen
John H Wilkins Coffee Company

Our senior partner, Howard Malloy, was the "rainmaker" and mainly responsible for managing the local office of Main & Company and developing additional cliental. He had relationships with senior executives at American Security & Trust Company, my former employer. John H. Wilkins Coffee Company was a local coffee manufacturer on Rhode Island Avenue and was owned and operated by John H. Wilkins Jr. His father had started the company in the early 1900's. And it was now under the son's ownership. They sold their coffee up and down the east coast, Philadelphia to Florida. They also maintained warehouses at strategic points up and down the east coast.

They wanted to expand their business and needed working capital. They had never borrowed and as a result they had never had a certified audit done. American Security & Trust was interested in being there banker but they required them to have a certified audit and annual audits thereafter. We were hired to do their first audit. The resident partner was assigned to be the partner in charge. I was now a semi-senior accountant so I was assigned to work with the resident partner and a new junior accountant was also assigned to the job.

The first thing that we did was to spend time touring their facility and understanding their manufacturing process. We also did an internal control assessment. Wilkins Coffee Company was the first to use the "Muppets" in television ads.

The manufacturing process appeared to be fairly simple. They purchased green coffee beans, roasted them, ground them, packaged them and then sold them. They had individual blends for restaurants and a different blend for the grocery stores. However as we looked more into the operation we found that they did not have counters at the end of the packaging lines and therefore did not have any idea of their actual production. They periodically took samples of their roasting process to determine the shrinkage from green coffee beans to finished coffee. We also noted that green coffee beans from different parts of the world had different shrinkage factors.

We found that they produced internal financial statements every quarter but in order to get cost of goods sold they had to take a complete inventory of green coffee and finished coffee. This was very labor intensive as all the warehouses had to be inventoried. They started with the previous inventory of green coffee, added purchases of green coffee and then subtracted ending green coffee inventory to get what was roasted. They used an average shrinkage percent to arrive at what was produced and added that to what was on hand at the last inventory and then subtracted the ending inventory to obtain the cost of goods sold. They then reviewed the gross margin to see if it was close to what it had been running.

This was a convoluted process with lots of opportunity for errors. If they knew what had been produced by putting counters on the lines it would have been much simpler and more accurate.

This was recommended by our resident partner but Mr. Wilkins wasn't willing to spend the money to add counters.

One of the first computers that IBM produced was their ECM machines, Electronic Accounting Machines. They were programmed by individually wiring a board to obtain what you wanted, inventory, sales, accounts payable, etc. There was a punch board for each program. Most companies had multiple boards, one for each application. However, Mr. Wilkins wasn't willing to spend the money buying multiple boards so each time that they changed a process they had to re wire the board. This was again a terrible use of time and caused many delays in obtaining accounting information. This was again because Mr. Wilkins chose not to spend the money.

One of the categories of inventory on the books was "Wine." The plant was quite old and the cellar was a natural wine cellar. It had stone walls and was cool and humid. When I asked about this I was told that the wine was in the cellar and we would need to inventory it. When I was taken to the cellar to see it, I couldn't believe what I was seeing. It was a huge area completely filled with cases and cases of French Wine.

The IRS had just completed an audit of the company and found that the wine was included as an inventory item, however it wasn't on site. Mr. Wilkins had moved it to his country home in Remington, VA (Chestnut Lawn). They told him that if it was going to be an asset of the company it needed to be at the company. As a result, Mr. Wilkins moved the entire inventory back to the factory. However, every day that he was at the plant he would take 2 or 3 bottles back home with him.

We completed our audit and were told that we would be their auditors for the next year also. Approximately two years later, they started to import green coffee from Africa. They had developed a roaster especially for these beans and the shrinkage was somewhat lower. The African beans were lower in price and the roasting process made them taste as good as the more expensive beans. We were calculating the cost of goods sold for a quarter and we were off by over $200,000. Cost of goods sold should have been lower but it was actually higher. This caused everyone to review everything from purchases to what had been roasted to final finished goods inventory.

We calculated the cost two and then three times. We could not determine what had happened. Had there been counters on the production line we would not have had this issue. There could have been any number of things that were wrong.

As a result we were fired and lost the accounting work for the Wilkins Coffee Company. My wife always knew when I was working at the coffee factory. The coffee smell got into my suit and I smelled like coffee.

This was a fun audit job well it lasted and I saw how management decisions had a direct impact on costs and operations.

Mr. Wilkins was eccentric to say the least. He came to the General Partner one year and asked him if he could buy a Rolls Royce. Howard Malloy told him he could do what he wanted. He said that he didn't want to have any problems with the IRS.

He had an issue during the IRS audit with his office furniture. It was all original Chinese Ming

Dynasty. The problem was that he was depreciating it when the IRS told him that it appreciated and he should not be depreciating it.

Chapter Fourteen
IRS Letter Ruling- El Paso Natural Gas

The Washington Office acted as the central depository for anything having to be processed through the IRS, or any other government Agencies.

Our El Paso, Texas office had as a client the El Paso Natural Gas Company. There was and still is a process whereby you can ask the IRS for a letter ruling on a tax issue. If approved you can then treat the item or items like that in the tax return.

The El Paso office had prepared something similar to a lawyers brief and sent it to the Washington Office to be walked through the IRS. I was given the task of handling this request in the Washington office. I had never done anything like this so I familiarized myself with the issue and what our El Paso Office was requesting.

We used Commerce Clearing House (CCH) tax service so I researched the issue and prepared my own summary.

I went to the IRS building in Wahington, D.C. to where requests were made. It was a long office with a counter and various IRS employees behind the counter. One of their employees was assigned to help me and I explained why I was there. They looked at the document that had been prepared by the El Paso office and then preceded to go to the back wall where there were copies of both CCH and Prentice Hall tax services.

When I saw what was happening I said to the individual that maybe I could help. I gave him the reference that I had reviewed. The employee pulled those references and after a short period came back and said that he agreed with our request. He then stamped and signed the request and handed it back to me and said I was good to go.

I have to admit that I was stunned by the entire process. But then I realized that they were no different than us. They used the same tax services and research to make decisions. What a shock but a useful experience.

I returned and sent the approved request to our El Paso office.

I doubt that you would be able today to walk a request through and it would probably take months to get an answer.

As the firm grew, I also grew in responsibilities. It was decided that the field of Management Information Systems (MIS) was positioned to have explosive growth in the next decade and that all offices should have one person assigned to that responsibility. I had continued my education at American University at night and I had taken a number of advanced courses in data processing, computers and management systems. As a result, the General Partner, Howard Malloy decided that I should be the one to represent our office. I attended a meeting at the Philadelphia Office and started to spend more time in this field then in the auditing field.

In 1966 I saw an ad for a MIS Director for a large regional C.P.A, firm in Atlanta, Ga. I applied for the position as I was finding that I was hitting the ceiling both in salary and in responsibility. I was only 28 and no one made resident partner until they were at least 35. I had been told by the General Partner that I was doing a great job and I just needed to take my time and I would be rewarded.

I didn't realize it but the protocol in public accounting firms was that you were not to seek out others working for another firm. If you received an inquiry, it was standard for one firm to contact the other firm. As a result the Atlanta firm contacted Howard Malloy and he blew a gasket.

He called me in and wanted to know what I was doing. I explained the situation but he was so emotional that there was really no explaining. Next the resident partner called me in and said that he was instructed to fire me immediately. He said that he had no choice but he didn't want to. I told him that I understood and that I was sorry that it had come to this.

When I joined Main & Co. as a junior accountant, I didn't realize it at the time, I was beginning a career that would take me through public accounting to the aerospace industry and on to an entrepreneur career over the next 45 years. The experience that I received in public accounting was the base for everything that was to come. I could have never realized how valuable it was for me to leave my Department of Commerce position and embark on a new phase, not only in my professional life but my personal life. My wife and I have just celebrated our 61st Wedding Anniversary. I could never have done it without Sharon at my side.

Chuck indicated that he would see that I received a month's severance pay and if he could help me he would. This was quite a rude awakening and especially since I had a wife and two small children at home, 4 and 3.

Fortunately, one of my associates at Main & Co. had left a few months before and had taken a job at Fairchild Hiller's Helicopter Division that had just relocated to

Rockville, MD from Palo Alto, CA. Manufacturing was being performed at the Fairchild Aircraft Division in Hagerstown, MD

Gary indicated that they were looking for an "Assistant to the Director of Finance" and if I was interested he would give my resume to the Personnel Department. I told him that I would like to meet with them and so within a week I had an interview. The interview went well and I was offered the job as the "Assistant to the Director of Finance" at an annual salary of $13,500 ($99,500 at 2016 dollars). This was a 42 percent increase from my public accounting salary and the work location was only 5 miles from my home. What could be better!

Public Accounting gave me the background and experience to move into industry. I couldn't have asked for a better opportunity to gain meaningful experience. I don't know if the same can be said of today's public accounting but I was grateful for the timing. My success in later companies could not have been possible without the background and experience I learned in public accounting. Looking back on that period, Howard Malloy did me a great favor but I didn't think so at the time. I never spoke to Howard after that time but I do appreciate the exposure and experience I gained from my almost five years there.

Public Accounting gave me the understanding of how different types of business operated. It allowed me the opportunity to interface with many different folks in many different businesses. I could have never received the experience and exposure if I had started work in an accounting department of a single company. I would have never had the opportunity to be exposed to the whole instead of just a portion of the business.

I know that today Public Accounting is not the same and there is much more compartmentalization. One might work only in taxes, or auditing or management services. Also, today you might only see one industry. You may only be assigned to banking, non-profits, manufacturing, healthcare, etc.

In the 1960's you had to be a generalist not a specialist. I would recommend anyone with a financial background to work in public accounting. It still is the best place to start your financial career.

The November 2016 issue of the Journal of Accountancy had an article entitled "Tips for first year auditors." There were seven tips and included: (1) Stay Calm, (2) Show up on time with a smile, (3) Be conscientious, (4)Know your limits, (5)Optimize client communication, (6) Get clarification upfront and (7) Enjoy the experience. These were as applicable 60 years ago as they are today. We were told then that if we didn't understand an assignment ask a question. It is better to do it right the first time then to barge ahead and not know what we were doing.

There are no "stupid questions." This is also something that I never forgot during my later career. The real world knowledge that you will receive in the first year is sometimes overwhelming but what an experience. We used to say that four or five years of public accounting experience was equivalent to twice that much in a corporate environment.

It was expected that before moving into industry that you should have at least 5 years of public accounting experience. I made it for 4 ½ years and can say that it was an extremely valuable 4 ½ years.

I believe today, as I did 60 years ago, that Public Accounting experience is the best prerequisite for a career in business. It gives you exposure to so many different aspects of accounting and finance in a short time. There is nowhere else that you could fine that.

I was fortunate that I had the opportunity to experience that. For a young person from a blue collar family, from central Pennsylvania, the road to success was education. It was then and still is today.

Many years later when I was fortunate to be a co-founder of AmeriChoice, a healthcare company for the Medicaid population, we found our best employees were those who were first generation college graduates. Our company had ethnic diversity in management as well as women that isn't found anywhere else today.

My experience working in Public Accounting formed the basis for the rest of my career, both working for major "for profit" corporations and also as an entrepreneur. It allowed me to interact with everyone from top management to the lowest clerk. It gave me an opportunity that I never knew existed growing up in Cherry Tree and Clearfield, Pa.

It also allowed me to realize that anyone can succeed if given a chance. You don't need to go to an Ivy League school, but you do need to work hard and do the best that you can in all things. Education is the answer, if you apply yourself.

The Journey
Part II

Chapter Fifteen

After almost 5 years in Public Accounting with Main Lafrentz; passing the C.P.A. exam the first time; completing my B.S.B.A. at American University and having a wife and two small children, I am starting down a new career path.

I had a month's severance from Main Lafrentz so time was of the essence. I enjoyed public accounting and thought that I might be able to make it a career, however "time in grade" was essential to become a partner regardless of your competency.

One of my associates at Main Lafrentz had left the firm a number of months ago to take a position in the accounting department of the Hiller Aircraft Division of Fairchild-Hiller Corporation. Gary Dowis had not taken the C.P.A. exam and had been told that there was no long term opportunity at Main Lafrentz and that he should consider a change.

The Hiller Aircraft Division had just relocated their administrative functions to Rockville, MD from Palo Alto, California. Their manufacturing was being done in Hagerstown, MD by the Aircraft Division of Fairchild. Hiller was augmenting their staffing in that only a few of their staff relocated. Hiller had been acquired by Fairchild and it was hopeful that they would be successful in winning a large government contract for light observation helicopters for the military. When they had not won the contract, a corporate decision was made to use that design for a commercial helicopter, the FH-1100, and produce it in Hagerstown at the Aircraft Division. A total of 100 were initially released to build.

Gary indicated that they were searching for an assistant to the Director of Finance. Since this was a division and not a separate corporation, the Director of Finance was the senior financial executive.

I put together a resume and Gary indicated that he would submit it to the employment office. In the meantime I started to consider other opportunities.

I received a call from the Director of Finance, Bert Fraylich, and an interview was set up. At the interview I met the Director of Finance and also the General Manager, George Attridge. They explained that this was a new position and that my background and experience fit their requirements. I received an offer within days at a compensation level 50% higher than what I had been making in public accounting.

After discussing this with my wife, Sharon, we decided to roll the dice and take the job. We were living in Rockville, MD at the time and their office was less than 10 miles from our home. It seemed like an ideal situation. It was July 1966 and I was now starting a new career in the corporate world. I had considered going to law school after completing my education at American University and had taken the LSAT but now a different journey was beginning.

I was in a staff position and assignments included special projects. My first assignment was to review the costs that were being transferred to our division by the Aircraft Division on a monthly basis. This required travel to Hagerstown, approximately 60 miles away. The Aircraft Division was housed in a facility that was still owned by the United States Air Force and had been used during World War II to produce aircraft for the United States.

This facility was over 1 million square feet and included an airfield. The Aircraft Division was producing commercial F-27 and FH-227 aircraft for regional airlines; FH-1100 helicopters for the commercial world; Porter short take-off and landing aircraft for hard to get areas of the world; flaps and spoilers for Boeing's 720 and 727 aircraft; retrofitting C-123 and C-129 aircraft for the military with jet assist take off pods; and working with Boeing on components for the super-sonic transport and 747 aircraft.

Fairchild had just made a significant investment in a bonding facility adjacent to its main plant and its primary use was for a new manufacturing technique, bonding aircraft components up to 50 feet long.

Employment at the Aircraft Division was approximately 4,500.

My first visit to the Aircraft Division was eye opening. I had never been in such a large manufacturing facility. I met with the Director of Finance, Al Brown, and was given a tour of the facility.

In a manufacturing facility such as this you had both direct and indirect costs. Each employee was either direct or indirect. Direct costs such as materials and labor that could be identified to a particular program were charged directly to it and then indirect costs were allocated as a percentage of the applicable direct costs. As an example, you had manufacturing direct and indirect; engineering direct and indirect; materials direct and indirect and then general and administrative that was a percentage of all the direct and indirect costs.

As I reviewed the cost transfers I found that the Aircraft Division was inflating the costs by not only charging the direct labor but also taking those employees that were considered indirect and charging them direct and then using the percentage for the indirect costs and charging them direct. In essence double counting.

It was obvious that this was intentional because it made the Aircraft Division's results look better.

I wrote a report and submitted it to both the Director of Finance and the General Manager. They had felt something was wrong but weren't positive until they saw the results of my analysis. They took this to Senior Management at the Corporation and changes were immediately made in costs transferred.

The Corporate Headquarters for Fairchild were at Hagerstown but a new Corporate Campus was being built in Germantown, MD, approximately half way between Washington and Hagerstown on I-70. Ed Uhl was CEO and Sherman Fairchild, the largest shareholder in IBM at the time, was Chairman. Ed Uhl was also the developer of the Bazooka during WW II. James Dresher was the General Manager of the Aircraft Division. The Corporate Executive Committee was actually the leader in strategy for the corporation and it was chaired by J. Bradford Wharton, a member of Fairchild's Board of Directors.

Brad was a C.P.A. and a brilliant accountant and strategist but also a bit eccentric. Most of the senior management of the corporation had been with the Martin Company, a defense contractor located outside of Baltimore, MD before coming to Fairchild after Sherman Fairchild had achieved control.

In the fall of 1966 rumors were developing that The Hiller Division was going to be merged into the Aircraft Division and that the administration functions would be relocating to Hagerstown. This actually made sense because as I learned more about the Aircraft Division I wondered why that didn't happen when it was first moved from Palo Alto. Stan Hiller, the founder of Hiller, was still a member of the Board of Directors of Fairchild and I assumed there were some political issues at the time.

It wasn't long before these rumors were confirmed and we were told that we would be moving at the beginning of 1967. This was somewhat disheartening to me but it made sense and was the right thing to do. I had no idea what I would be doing because now there would be two of everyone in finance and it was obvious that decisions would have to be made about staffing.

I decided to see what was going to happen and Sharon and I made the decision that I would commute to Hagerstown daily for the foreseeable future. None of this would have been possible without a wonderful woman, Sharon, taking care of the home front. We had two children with a third on the way.

Shortly after the first of the year, 1967, Brad Wharton visited the Aircraft Division and asked me to head up a new project, under his direction, the first Corporate Long Range Plan. The Aircraft Division was selected as the prototype since it was the largest corporate division.

Long Range Planning/Forecasting was just starting to be implemented in Corporate America and Brad wanted Fairchild to be in the forefront of this new tool. The approach was to look at a five year horizon and review current business and future business to determine resources necessary to continue to grow the business.

Brad also wanted to try to assign all costs to a project, direct and indirect, as specifically as possible. This would allow the corporation to know what projects were truly profitable and what were not.

In 1967 we had an IBM 360-40 computer but everything was run in batch mode. There were no personal computers and no software that would enable this planning function. Everything was done manually, using 7, 14, 21 and 28 column accounting worksheets.

One of the useful items that I learned in public accounting was to understand what you were trying to accomplish and then set up your worksheets so that they would allow you to reach your objective. This was extremely useful in this project.

I would work on this project during the week and then meet with Brad somewhere in Washington, DC the following week. Brad was usually in Washington DC every week. His favorite restaurant was The Occidental Grill on Pennsylvania Ave. I would meet him there for dinner and we would review what I had done. He would then suggest changes and another idea would develop and I would go back and modify the approach. Many times he would write on a cloth napkin, a new idea, and I would take the napkin with me as I changed the approach.

These meetings went on for at least three months until Brad was satisfied that we had done as much as we could. This was then implemented throughout the entire corporation. This was an exciting time and an incredible learning experience.

During this period there were a number of organizational and management changes being made throughout the division. The Corporate Offices were moved to Germantown and James Dresher, the General Manager, moved also to the corporate office. Charles Blaney was hired from Martin –Orlando to be the new General Manager. The merger of the Aircraft Division and the Hiller Division quickly showed where the strengths and weaknesses were in the organization.

The Controller of the Aircraft Division had a number of issues that were obvious. He didn't provide leadership to the finance organization. He had a large bank type adding machine in his office and he would add up the columns of the computer reports daily. He very seldom interacted with the finance employees.

I knew that I couldn't work for him and having finished the long range planning project I knew that it was time to consider what I wanted to do with the rest of my life.

One Friday afternoon, I was called into the office of the Director of Finance, George Attridge. George had been the General Manager of the Hiller Diviison in Rockville and upon the merger of the two divisions, George had been made the Director of Finance, as he had a cost accounting background. Brad Wharton was also in attendance.

I was asked how I was and what I thought of the current finance structure. I have always answered honestly and I said that I felt there were serious issues in the management of finance. I was then asked if I could have any job in finance, what would that be? Again, I answered honestly and said that I would like to be the Controller. George said that is fine. As of Monday morning you are the new Controller. I was shocked and without words. I asked whether he was serious and he said he was. Brad said that they were happy with what I had been doing and they realized that there needed to be a change. I asked what was going to happen to the current controller and they said that he would work in Kenny Harp's Estimating shop.

When I arrived home, I told Sharon what had occurred and said that we were moving to Hagerstown. She was pregnant at the time with Stacy. A change was happening. I had a new position, we had to sell our house and buy a new one and with a new baby on the way. Always a trooper, Sharon said well I guess we need to get started. I was 29 years of age with a new challenge ahead.

The first thing that I did upon becoming Controller was to get rid of the old "bank adding machine." The former Controller's administrative assistant was a huge help as I embarked on trying to make the accounting department more efficient. Evie was old enough to be my Mother and she wanted me to be successful. She had been at Fairchild for over 20 years and knew where "all the bodies were buried."

All hourly employees were paid by cash while salary employees were paid by check. I had 25 people preparing cash envelopes weekly for the employees and then having the employee sign for their cash envelope. A Brinks truck would bring the cash in once a week.

Shortly after I took over as Controller I saw that the accounts payable department was very behind in processing invoices. I told the Accounts Payable Supervisor to use some of the payroll employees to help when they were finished with the payroll. Within a day, I had a visit from the Director of the Personnel Department. He had a number of pink slips that were grievances against me filed by the Union Stewart. I was told that transferring employees between departments was against the Union Contract. I had over 250 people in the accounting department and there were many inefficiencies. I was unable to transfer people between departments because of the union contract.

We had the UAW Union at Fairchild and the union contract was extremely strong. The accounting department's hourly workers fell under this agreement. An accountant that was in the accounts payable department could not be transferred, even temporarily, into another accounting department such as payroll without being in violation of the union contract.

I told the Personnel Manager that I would like to meet with the Union Steward. He said this was not possible because all union affairs had to go through Personnel. I said that wasn't satisfactory and I proceeded to find out who the Union Stewart was that had filed the grievances and asked for him to meet with me. A meeting was arranged and I told him that the situation with accountants in the union agreement wasn't workable.

I needed the ability to move folks around between accounting functions and if that wasn't possible he left me with no choice but to lay off accountants in areas that had not enough work and hire new employees for the other areas where there was a need. Maryland was a "right to work" state and new hires weren't required to join the union if they didn't want to. I said "I didn't think this would sit well with their union employees that would have to be laid off."

He agreed and said that they would be open to changing this section in the next agreement and that they would not object to my moving folks around to where there was a requirement.

I told the Personnel Representative that an agreement had been reached and they were shocked. However, our agreement was a common sense arrangement for both parties.

Once this situation was resolved, I looked at how we could eliminate cash payrolls. This would allow us to be more efficient and reduce manpower. In researching this issue I found that one of the main reasons this hadn't been tackled before was that many of the employees did not have a bank checking account and their spouses had no idea how much money they made. The employees didn't want this to change. The spouses received so much cash from the employee weekly.

We had conversations with a number of the local banks and we were able to reach a satisfactory outcome. The banks would cash the employees' checks and give them a no cost checking account as well. Even if the employee didn't want a checking account they would continue to cash their checks. We received an ok from the Union and implemented this program successfully.

In working through this change I had meetings with the manufacturing department and found that one of the major problems was that work orders could not be tracked without doing a physical inventory. This was time consuming and wasn't current. A working group consisting of IT, manufacturing, and accounting personnel was established to find a solution that would be cost and operational effective.

A solution was developed that included using the time card machines and punch cards that went with the work order and as it arrived in a department or left a department the cards were processed nightly and daily reports showed where the work order was and how many hours were spent in that department on them. This became useful later as we then used this to compare to budget on almost a real time basis. This was not only helpful for finance but it was also useful to the manufacturing department. A win win for all.

When the Corporate Office relocated to their new facilities in Germantown, MD. A new General Manager was hired as the existing General Manager went to Corporate. Charles Blaney, a Facilities Manager for Martin – Orlando was hired as the new General Manager.

Charley was a manufacturing expert having spent his career from the ground floor up in manufacturing. Charley wasn't a college graduate but he had an innate sense of manufacturing issues and how to solve them.

He spent a few weeks getting to know the organization and taking daily walks around the manufacturing floor, talking to both supervisors and workers. He asked me to accompany him on these walks and it was an incredible experience. It helped me understand the relationship between finance and manufacturing to a degree that would not be possible without this. In the 1960's a number of books were written about "Managing by Walking Around." There is no question that if you want to get to the bottom of work issues this is the most effective method.

One of the things that Charley determined was wrong was that there was poor morale among the work force. Parts weren't where they should be when they should be and sometimes no one knew where they were. This contributed to overruns in cost, labor and materials. They changes that we were implementing in labor reporting and movement of work orders should help and they did.

However, 250 FH-1100 helicopters had now been released to production and they were not being completed on a timely basis. As a result customers were cancelling their orders and an inventory of new FH-1100's was accumulating on the tarmac.

After a few weeks of reviewing the manufacturing process Charley called the facilities manager, the manufacturing manager and me into his office and said that he wanted to have an open house for the employees and their families, including children. There would be a company sponsored picnic, music and games for the children.

Many of the programs that were in the facility had secret or top secret government clearances attached to them. There was some push back that what he wanted to do wasn't going to be possible. Charley said that the government affairs folks would be assigned to find a way to make this happen.

In order to get ready for this he also wanted all work areas to be cleaned up. In addition he wanted to paint walkway outlines throughout the plant and he wanted the steam pipes, electric pipes etc. painted different colors to differentiate them. The facilities manager said this would be expensive and he thought it was crazy. Charley would not accept no for an answer and said it had to be done.

Many of the managers thought this was crazy and costly but everyone participated and the work was completed on time and the family outing was held on a Saturday. It was a great success and it paid off in dividends more than anyone could have predicted. Production improvement increased dramatically and employee morale increased significantly. I was learning more than I could ever realize about manufacturing and employee morale and how to get things done.

Fairchild had been delivering the new FH-227 turboprop to regional airlines for a few years. Airlines such as Southern, Ozark, Piedmont, Pacific, Mohawk, Allegheny, etc. and had taken in trade some of the old prop planes that they had been flying.

When I took over as Controller I realized that we had over 56 of those trade in's and they were sitting on the tarmac at Hagerstown. They were started weekly, tires rotated periodically including a minimum amount of maintenance.

The value on the books was approximately $10-12 million dollars in 1966 dollars. In today's dollars that would be over $100 million. This array of airplanes included DC-3's, F-27's, Constellations and DC-6's. These aircraft had been accumulated over a number of years and nothing was being done to sell them. Pat Coleman had recently been hired as the Used Aircraft Marketing Manager. Pat had come from Curtis Wright where he had been used parts manager.

I was assigned to work with Pat on developing a strategy to dispose of these aircraft at the highest price possible. In addition, Brad Wharton had realized that we were not depreciating these aircraft and directed us to start depreciating the cost on the books over 60 months, thereby gaining a tax advantage.

Pat thought that the salvage value might be worth more than an outright sale. Pat thought that we should plan to visit a number of aircraft salvage facilities to determine if that made any sense. We set up a schedule to visit about three of the major salvage yards for aircraft as well as a few aircraft brokers. We started in Florida, went to California and then Las Vegas, Nevada.

We quickly determined that salvaging the aircraft for used parts was not economically feasible. There was a glut of used parts for these aircraft and therefore not much of a demand, thus depressing the value. A number of the brokers that we met with thought that there was a market to sell the whole aircraft, but that continuing to keep them in Hagerstown would lead to more maintenance issues.

We met with a friend of Pat's, Lloyd Percell of Cargo Air Service in Las Vegas. Lloyd had a fixed base operation at McCarron Air Field and had a contract with Livermore Laboratory in California to fly people and cargo from California to their various test facilities in Nevada and New Mexico. There was room at McCarron to store the aircraft and it was thought that folks would love to come to Las Vegas to see them. The desert environment would help to maintain them.

Upon returning to Hagerstown we prepared a report and recommended that we move all of the aircraft to Las Vegas and enter into a brokerage deal with Cargo Air Service. This was approved and we put together a plan to move them.

We hired pilots from the Air Force Base at Andrews AFB to pilot them and set about a schedule. These aircraft had not been flown for over two years. We had aircraft down all over the United States, mostly due to oil leaks, but we did finally get them all relocated.

We were able to get these aircraft all sold, mostly to South America organizations. In the meantime, I made monthly trips to Las Vegas to inventory the aircraft and determine marketability. This was a new experience, seeing Las Vegas in the 1960's. I was also learning a different field then straight finance. I was involved in "Management Decisions."

We leased some of the aircraft with an option to purchase. One of these arrangements was with an organization in Alaska owned by Jim McGofflin. Jim was a graduate of the Colorado School of Mines and had moved to Fairbanks to start a bush airline for hunters and fishermen. As a result he also had developed an airfield with one gravel runway in the upper northwest area of Alaska. When oil was discovered by British Petroleum in 1967 he received a contract to fly people and equipment to that part of Alaska because of his airfield.

We leased one of the used F-27's to him so that he could move folks from Anchorage to Fairbanks as an intrastate airline. However, Wien and Air Alaska soon cut their prices requiring him to stop operating. We had leased the F-27 to him and then arranged financing for him through GE Capital. The purchase agreement was sent but he never signed or returned it. We attempted to contact him but he would not respond. It was decided that Lloyd Percell and I would make a trip to Fairbanks to determine what was happening.

I flew to Las Vegas and then we flew to Seattle and then on to Fairbanks. We arrived at around 2:00 A.M. on a July 1967 morning. We had no idea where we were going to stay. We hired a taxi and told the driver that we needed a room and he said no problem. He called his dispatcher and arrangements were made. In the meantime he received a call that he needed to stop by the University of Alaska and pick up a passenger.

This was a new experience. The passenger was a drunk student and he was to deliver him to a location in Fairbanks. We arrived at our hotel. It was only a few rooms over a restaurant that appeared to be from about the 1920's. We were handed a key and we were on our own. The next morning we were met by someone who called himself Red Boucher, Mayor of Fairbanks. He really was the Mayor of Fairbanks and had been sent by Jim to pick us up and take us to his office at the airfield. Red worked for Jim. "Red" Boucher would later become Lieutenant governor of Alaska from 1970-1974.

When we meet Jim, he had mounts of every type of big game that is found in Alaska in his office. Included was a full mounted Grizzly Bear standing in the corner of his office.

When we got down to business we learned what had happened to his intrastate airline but he said that he was still going to purchase the F-27 because he had just signed a contract with British Petroleum (BP) to fly all of their personnel and equipment to the North Slope. BP had struck oil. This was a significant development and would mean a great deal to him as he had the only airstrip in the area.

We left Alaska knowing that we had a deal. Iin a few weeks all papers were signed and we were paid. In addition, Jim purchased another F-27 and also a number of C-130's.

On our way home I flew through Las Vegas. Lloyd asked me to meet with Cliff Jones. He said that Cliff was an investor in Cargo Air Services. We met with Mr. Jones to discuss the oil find in Alaska.

Mr. Jones opened a desk drawer and took out a telephone and picked up the receiver. He was connected directly to a brokerage house. Later I learned that he had been the Lieutenant Governor of Nevada, an attorney and also a major investor in casinos. He had also been implicated in the Continental Vending Machine fiasco with Bobby Baker, a former aide to Senator Lyndon Johnson. He was never prosecuted. Las Vegas in the 1960's was an interesting place.

I was scheduled to be in Las Vegas on one of my monthly trips at the same time that the Helicopter Association of America was having their annual meeting. Charley Blaney was scheduled to address the meeting and he asked me to stay and join him. We had a number of our FH-1100 helicopters on display. All of our marketing personnel were pilots. Ed Eckhard was a manger in the marketing department and had been a pilot in the Vietnam War in the 1960's.

Ed suggested that we take one of the helicopters out into the desert and to Lake Meade. I had an 8 mm movie camera with me and I set up front in the left seat. A helicopter pilot sits in the right seat. The bubble was tinted and acted as a filter for my home movie. We spent the afternoon putting the helicopter through its paces and I was able to get some terrific pictures.

On one of my trips to Las Vegas, our marketing personnel had brought a helicopter for a Texas rancher and oil man. It was to be on display and then delivered. The major issue was that the paperwork had not been prepared. We had received a significant deposit but there was still over $50,000 due. The price of an FH-1100 was in excess of $125,000 in 1967 but over $1 million in today's dollars. The marketing representative came to me and said that the purchaser wanted to take his helicopter home, I said ok. I took a piece of paper and wrote a receipt for the helicopter and had the owner sign it. I told the marketing rep to have the department get all paperwork ready and send to him.

A week later I received a check in the mail with my hand written receipt, for the balance and a thank you for being understanding. In those days a handshake still meant something.

In the summer we had a plant shutdown for two weeks. All employees were to take a vacation during this period. In a production facility this was the most economical way to handle vacations. Each department had a skeleton crew on site and anyone who had more than two weeks vacation could schedule the balance later in the year.

I was designated to be in charge of the entire facility for the shutdown of 1967. During this period the parts department had received a call from Mohawk Airlines that they had an aircraft on the ground (AOG). Whenever one of our customers had an AOG situation we would always do everything that we could to get them what they required to get the aircraft back in the air. I was notified of the situation and asked what I wanted to do. I said we needed to make every effort to determine the problem and get them what they needed as soon as possible. The paperwork could come later. We had to call in some employees but we were able to get what they needed to them in a few days. Mission accomplished.

A few days after the plant was back in operation at full force, I was called into the General Manager's office and asked what happened on the Mohawk AOG? I told him the story and was surprised when he handed me a letter he had received from the President of Mohawk commending me for the effort we made to satisfy their issue. I was pleasantly surprised.

As we became more proficient in working with the various departments to solve their needs, we also were able to gain more visibility into the cost drivers and the financial needs of the division. It was a win for all.

In reviewing the accounting department's needs, I had two supervisors that had transferred from Hiller that were competent but the other managers were marginal. I knew that we needed some strength in a few areas and so we did a personnel search for a Senior Cost Accountant and a Senior General Accountant.

We were able to find two individuals with the experience that I was looking for. Neither had a college degree but one had been at B.F. Goodrich for over 10 years in their accounting department and one had been with another defense contractor for about the same amount of time. Doug Stover came from Goodrich and Dick Wellemeyer came from the other company, both in Ohio. Both were smart and hard working. They had the experience even if they didn't have a college degree.

I had my team. John Donlan and Syd Griffith were from Hiller, Gary Dowis had been in public accounting with me and Doug and Dick that I had just hired. The old axiom that when hiring always hire someone who is smarter and wiser than you was never more true. My entire staff was older than me by at least 10 years but I treated them with respect and they did the same for me.

To try to keep some balance between work and family, we found a mountain cabin for sale about an hour away in Pennsylvania near Mont Alto. There had been a TB Sanatorium there at one time. The cabin was basic but was on three acres in the woods. Our children were young but we enjoyed getting away. This led us to invest in some additional undeveloped mountain land between Gettysburg and Chambersburg Pa. There were a number of rock walls on the property and it was said that there had been a Civil War battle on the property.

Another land investment was approximately 90 acres on a mountaintop north of Thurmont, MD, where Camp David is located. When we relocated to Connecticut we sold all and broke-even.

The F-27 and FH-227 were Fokker Aircraft designs (a Dutch Company). Fokker had just come out with a twin jet design for a 40 to 50 passenger aircraft called the F-

28. Ed Uhl, the President of Fairchild, always wanted to compete with Boeing and he saw this as the opportunity. A deal was struck with Fokker and we were going to embark on a 100 airplane lot of F-228's. This plane would be larger than the F-28 and have a new set of avionics and new engines. The engines would be designed by Rolls Royce and Collins would design the avionics. Cost estimates put the price at approximately $2.4 million per aircraft. This was approximately 2 ½ times that of the FH-227.

The market was expected to be the regional airlines. George Attridge, the current Director of Finance, was selected to be the Program Director on this project. It was to be a functional project with procurement handled within the project but manufacturing through the manufacturing department. I was called into the General Manager's office and told that George was moving over to take charge of this new program and that I was being promoted to Director of Finance. I now had responsibility for accounting, estimating, and information technology. This was a significant move for me and one that I was happy to make.

As I moved into this new position I also had to make some personnel decisions. I needed a Controller and decided that I needed to go outside the company to find one. Also, there had been some issues with the Director of the IT organization and after reviewing that organization, I realized that I had to replace that individual.

This was one of the most difficult decisions in my career. The Director of IT had just returned from having a heart attack. He was old enough to be my father but he wasn't getting the job done. In addition, there were some rumors that he was harassing some of the women employees in data entry on the night shift. After an investigation, I found that to be true and so I fired him. Ken Kaser was second in command and after reviewing his background I decided to make him the new head of IT. That was a bold decision but one that worked.

Ken also did not have a college degree but he had learned computers in the Air Force and was well schooled in manufacturing.

We had a company newspaper and my promotion was included in the next edition. Shortly after publication, Charley Blaney called me into his office and asked me how old was I. I told him I had just turned 30. He was shocked and said I didn't realize you were that young. I asked him if that was a problem? He said no and I asked him "would that have made a difference" if he knew that before I was promoted. He laughed and said "no and said get out and get to work."

We looked at financial and manufacturing issues and set out to improve systems that would help all departments, not just finance. We implemented a new cost system, improved payroll by working with a local bank to set up free checking accounts for all employees and going to direct deposit for payroll. Many improvements to our collective bargaining agreement with the UAW was made at the next negotiation.

In the meantime we successfully integrated the Republic Aviation Company into the Aircraft Division (Fairchild had recently acquired Republic).

We had a private dining facility for all mangers in our operation. This was very economical and kept the managers at the facility and reduced any loss time. It also allowed the managers from different departments to communicate with each other in a non- adversary-

environment. This was quite common among aerospace companies in the 1950's and early 1960's.

The GM called me into his office one day and advised me that Arthur Godfrey would be visiting our facility. Arthur Godfrey had a very successful radio show and was a serious aviation individual. He had his own plane and was a qualified pilot. Our marketing personnel was going to take an FH-1100 to pick him up at his estate in Leasburg, VA, about 60 miles away, and bring him to the plant for a visit and lunch. I was to join him for lunch. Arthur Godfrey was quite a celebrity but during lunch he was obnoxious and foul mouthed and not pleasant to be around. It was not a pleasant situation. That was the last we heard from him.

As the planning developed for the F-228, it was decided that since our market was the regional airlines, we needed to promote that. It was decided that we would build a full scale prototype and also create a separate dining facility for the airline executives that we hoped to sell the aircraft to.

Cost estimates were prepared and they indicated that the cost of the prototype (in wood) would amount to approximately $750,000 plus another $300,000 for the restaurant. The budgets were approved at corporate and production was commenced. We proceeded to build a full scale prototype as well as an attached high end French restaurant. This was to be a marketing tool. However it was never utilized.

As to the program, it was estimated that we would sell the F-228 at a base price of approximately $2.4 million each in the first lot of 100 aircraft. There were significant engineering and development costs since new engines were to be designed and built by Rolls Royce, new avionics by Collins and a new triple slotted flap that was to permit shorter takeoffs and landings. Most of the same vendors would be used for components of the aircraft that Folker was using.

This was to mitigate costs and development costs. In the final analysis, we would primarily be assembling the components from world-wide manufacturers into the final product.

Contracts were issued and work began. After a year we had received only 2 orders (from Pacific Air) and the first aircraft components were in the mating gigs. It was obvious that this project was going to be a bust. It was early in 1968 and this project could sink the corporation. Decisions had to be made and it was obvious that this project needed to be cancelled. Finally, a decision was made to cancel this project and negotiate cancellation agreements with all of the vendors began.

We also had to look at our personnel and start to reduce manpower throughout all departments. As a result the first reduction was to go from approximately 4,500 employees to 3,000. In achieving this I laid off over 100 financial types in one afternoon. We were in a doomsday environment.

At the same time, I received an unexpected call from a personnel recruiter wanting to know if I would be interested in discussing a Controller's position with Air America. This position was in Taiwan and they would provide living quarters for the family as well.

Sharon and I now had three children with the oldest being 6 and the youngest a few months. I also knew that Air America was a CIA front, as we had sold a number of modified Porter STOL aircraft to them to be used in Vietnam.

It didn't take me long to say thanks but no thanks. I didn't see this as a favorable career move.

In a few weeks, I received another call and was told that General Dynamics was interested in talking to me. They were one of the largest aerospace companies, at the time, with operations throughout the United States and Canada. They were headquartered in New York City. I said that I would talk with them. A meeting was set up and I flew to New York City to meet with the Corporate Controller, David Thomas.

In my meeting with Dave Thomas I was told that they were looking for a Controller for their San Diego operation, Convair. They explained how they were set up and that the Corporate office was relatively small, approximately 200. The Corporate Office was at 49th and Rockefeller Center. We had lunch with a few of his direct reports at the restaurant overlooking the skating rink. During lunch I was asked what my schedule was like for the afternoon. I said that I was returning home. He asked would I have time to meet with their consultant, Rohr, Hibbler & Repoggel. I was aware that major corporations were using outside psychological consulting companies to evaluate new hires. General Dynamics was also. I said that I would be happy to meet with them. David left the table and made a call and when he returned he said that I was to meet at their offices at 2:00.

After lunch I took a taxi and went to their offices. I met with one of the executives at RH&R and we talked generally about my personal background and business experience. He was primarily interested in my personal background. He also had me take some elementary psychological tests including an ink blot test. When we completed the interview he asked me if I had any questions. I said yes, I had one. I said that he didn't look much older than I and that it was obvious that he wasn't expecting me and that he didn't know anything about me, so what made him qualified to make an assessment of me that could impact my career. He laughed and said that he had never been asked that before and that he couldn't answer me. I thanked him and caught the next plane home.

The following week I received a call from Dave Thomas offering me the job at a salary of $23,500 (over $160,000) in today's dollars and $7,000 over my current salary at the time. He also said that I would need to spend about three months in New York City, learning the corporate nuances and then I would move to San Diego. They would pay for all my expenses in New York City and all transportation costs to and from. I said that I needed a few days to discuss this with my wife.

Fairchild was in a tail spin at the time and it didn't appear that anything was going to change in the near future. Sharon and I discussed the pros and cons and we decided that it was the smart career move. In November 1968, I started my new job at General Dynamics.

On my first day of work I was assigned an office on the 29th floor overlooking the Plaza at Rockefeller Center with a view of the Hudson River. The office was quite large and had two windows that actually opened. One day a window washer came in my office, closed the office door and went to a window and opened it and reached out with a safety harness and latched onto a bolt in the outside wall, swung out and then attached his harness to the other side, closed the window and washed it and then came in and proceeded to the second window. When he was finished I stopped him as he was leaving and told him they didn't pay him enough to do that. He said that sometimes the bolts in the outside wall would be loose but that was why he pulled on it before he went out.

The new buildings had a sleigh that moved up and down on a rail since the windows didn't open.

Another day the USS United States was making its maiden voyage and was arriving to a fireboat reception with water being sprayed. I had a first row view.

My commute to New York began on a Monday morning, taking a commuter airline from Hagerstown to Baltimore where I would take an Allegheny flight to New York's LaGuardia Airport. I would then take a taxi to the office. I would leave home at about 7:00 A.M. and I would arrive at the office between 9:30 and 10:00 A.M. On Friday I would reverse the commute arriving in Hagerstown at about 7:30 P.M.

During the week I would stay at a hotel in the city. Initially, I stayed at the Summit Hotel that was on the east side of town in the 60's. This was my preference but if I wasn't able to get a reservation there I would stay at the New York Hilton. It was somewhat inconvenient moving every week but there wasn't another satisfactory solution.

On my first week of commuting, the corporate travel office contacted me and wanted to know if there was another flight I could take. I said no and asked them why were they interested? They said that they wanted all of their Corporate Staff to fly first class, wherever possible. That was a nice perk but not one that I would be able to enjoy.

In early January 1969, Amtrak started a high speed train from New York to Washington D.C. with a stop at Baltimore. I decided to try this since Penn Station wasn't far from my office. Also, traffic on a Friday evening could be difficult. I found that I could actually make the same time on Friday as I had been but with less difficulty. This became my new mode of transportation.

Initially, I was oriented into the reporting that the operations provided the Corporate Office and their reviews. The Corporate Controller had Corporate Accounting and a separate analytical section comprised of Financial Analysts with M.B.A.'s. There was one analyst assigned to each division and/or operations. I was the only one with a C.P.A. and experience in a manufacturing operation.

My first assignment was to rework the monthly reports that came from the operations and the monthly reports that went to the Corporate Board of Directors. The thought was that we needed to simplify the reports without losing the important information. I worked with the IT department at the Fort Worth facility where we were producing F-111's for the United States Air Force. Fort Worth had a complete graphics group and in a short period of time we were able to redesign and produce a new report that everyone agreed to. After this I was assigned to head up the Analysis Group and to be the face of recruiting new analysts. We recruited two to three new M.B.A.'s annually. The final voice on who we should hire was RH&R. I found that strange but this was the way recruiting was moving. I found it interesting in that the approach was to hire M.B.A.'s at the Corporate Office and then after a year to two years send them out to an operation in charge of a department.

I always felt that the better way would to put them at the operations level and the move them to a corporate analytical position after a few years.

After three months it didn't appear that I was getting any closer to being transferred to San Diego. I decided to have a talk with Dave Thomas. Dave said that they were making some changes and that they decided that I was actually more valuable in the corporate office and they wanted me to stay in New York and take over all of the accounting functions for the corporation. I said that that was a very generous offer but that I missed being in an operating entity. I was still only 30 and I didn't particularly want to live in New York City. Dave asked me to consider this and I said that I would.

I discussed this with Sharon and as always she said it is your decision. I said I would look at housing alternatives in the New York area and then we would decide. In the meantime we had sold our home in Hagerstown and had moved into an apartment, anticipating a move to San Diego. The housing market was getting difficult and we felt that if we had an opportunity to sell we should.

After looking at the housing choices in the New York area and the commute time, I knew that I didn't want to be in the New York office. I told Dave that I didn't think that would work for us and he said that he understood but that they didn't want to lose me and so if I would continue to commute that they would find something else for me in one of their other operations.

On one of my commutes to New York I ran into Wayne Hudson who had been Director of Manufacturing at Fairchild but had now taken a position with Kaman Aerospace Corporation in Bloomfield, CT. He asked what I was doing and after discussing the current situation he mentioned that Kaman was looking for a Controller. Kaman Aerospace had just been spun off from Kaman Corporation. If I had any interest he would discuss it with the new President, Jack Anderson. I said that it couldn't hurt to look into it. When I got to work I decided to do research on Kaman.

Kaman was a helicopter manufacturer for the Navy and also a sub-contractor for Lockheed (C-5A) and

Grumman (F-14). They had approximately 3,500 employees at Kaman Aerospace.

They also had a separate company, Kaman Sciences in Colorado Springs, Co. and a ball bearing company, KACARB, and an aircraft fixed base operation in Hartford, CT. They had made the decision to spin Kaman Aerospace off as a separate company, wholly owned by Kaman Corporation. Charley Kaman, an engineer, had started this company and still controlled it even though it was a public corporation.

Kaman Aerospace had an offsite plant in Moosup, CT where detail parts and sub-assemblies were made, and a final assembly and test facility at Bloomfield, CT.

Kaman Aerospace had just recently been spun off and was the largest of their companies with over 3,500 employees.

I was called by the President of Kaman Aerospace, Jack Anderson, and an interview was set up. I went to their headquarters in Bloomfield, CT, outside of Hartford. I met Jack and the Corporate CFO, Bruce Clark. I also meet Charley Kaman, the founder of Kaman. I felt that it was a successful interview. I was pleasantly impressed by what I saw. I also found out that my old mentor from Fairchild, Brad Wharton, was a consultant to Charlie Kaman.

The following week I received a call from Jack Anderson with a verbal offer to become Controller at a salary of $26,500 (about $238,000) in today's dollars. I thanked him and said that I would like to discuss this with my wife and I would let him know within a few days. I called Sharon and as always she said it is up to you. I also called Brad Wharton. I told Brad what had happened and he said that he knew and that I needed to take the position because he had recommended me to Charley and Jack. I told Brad thanks and that I was going to call and accept the position.

I told Dave Thomas that I had received an offer from Kaman Aerospace and that I planned to accept it. I told him that General Dynamics had been more than fair in our relationship but that I wanted to get back to an operational position. Dave said that he understood but that he didn't know much about Kaman and would I allow him to do some due diligence on Kaman before I accepted the position. I thought that he was being very generous and I agreed.

He came back to me in a few days and said that Kaman was apparently a quality company and he could fine nothing bad about them. I thanked him, gave him my two weeks notice, and accepted the position at Kaman.

In May 1969, we moved from Hagerstown to Bloomfield, CT. I rented a house for a year in the same neighborhood that Kaman's Director of Personnel lived. We would be less than 6 miles away from the office. This would allow us time to look at other options to purchase.

My responsibilities at Kaman included accounting, cost accounting, budgeting, cost estimating and MIS. One of the first projects delegated to me was whether we should allow Lockheed to exercise their option on C-5A components even though they had missed the option date.

Kaman was a producer of flaps, spoilers and ailerons for the C-5A program and they were losing money on the first contract. The initial contract contained options and dates on which those options had to be exercised as well as option prices. I gathered my Director of Cost Accounting and Director of Cost Estimating together and advised them that we were going to put together an analysis of where we were on the program and what we had lost and what the next option quantity would probably cost and then compare that to the contract. We had less than a week to complete this. For some reason, Lockheed had failed to exercise their option by days.

As we examined the program in depth, it was obvious that a detailed analysis had not been done previously. When we were finished it looked as though we would lose millions of dollars if we were to except the exercise of the option. We were using the accounting approach that all losses must be recognized immediately even though cost may not have been incurred. This meant that upon the acceptance of the option we would have to write off the expected contract losses.

I reviewed this with Jack Anderson and he said we needed to meet with Charley Kaman. We went upstairs to Charley's office with Bruce Smith, Kaman Corporation's CFO. Jack and I gave my presentation and it was not well received. The Corporation's CFO was silent and Charley said to him, "How could this had happened?" Charley said that he needed some time to think about this.

I thought that being the messenger of bad news may have cost me my job after only a few weeks on the job.

The next day, Charley called us back and said that he had discussed this with Brad Wharton, his outside financial consultant, and that Brad had agreed that Kaman should not allow the option to be exercised and that a letter from our attorney would be sent to Lockheed indicating that they had missed the option date and that we would like to continue doing business but the price for the exercise of the option would have to be renegotiated.

Within weeks, Lockheed called and said that they were willing to renegotiate the contract. After some tense negotiations we were able to reach a satisfactory agreement. We went on to perform the contract at a profit.

Kaman was suffering from not having systems and procedures to allow the operating departments to financially know where they stood. Finance needed to be more management oriented then green eye shade accountants.

Engineering was starting to use the GE Timesharing system for design analysis and the cost estimating department was starting to use it for analytical analysis on costs of a project. In addition, we also had an IBM 360-40 computer system that was being used for various operations. Similar to Fairchild, there was no integrated system to monitor work packages in manufacturing and cost incurred. There was also no one in charge of the MIS department.

After reviewing resources and capabilities and looking at personnel it was obvious that I needed some heavy weights. I contacted Ken Kaser, Doug Stover and Richard Welleymeyer. They were all still at Fairchild. I wanted to know whether they were interested in moving. I had recruited all of them and I knew that they had the qualifications to move Kaman into the next decade. All said yes and I now had the nucleus of an outstanding staff. There were also two key employees at Kaman that augmented this finance management staff and had the corporate knowledge to move it forward. Walter Kozlow was one. Walter had worked his way up from manufacturing to cost estimating. In later years, Walter would become President of Kaman Aerospace.

As we reviewed the cost structure, I realized that we were using the GE Timesharing System more and more. The more we used it the more it cost us. We had terminals connected directly to a main frame computer via a direct line to their computer location. This was a very early version of the internet but for specialized use.

As we reviewed our use, we looked into alternatives and found that we could purchase a computer system, contract for their software and our costs would be fixed no matter how many users we had or how much we used it. We could also sell time to others. The hardware was Hewlett-Packard.

We found that educational facilities were using their own systems and decided to visit a few to see how they were operating. The University of Maine and the University of Alabama were two that HP suggested that we visit. Visits were arraigned and we found that having our own system was the most cost effective and made operational sense. We received an ok and entered into an arrangement with HP and installed the system and set up a small organization to market and operate it. Within a year we were cost neutral as we were able to obtain enough outside business to pay for the system.

One of our major sub-contracts was with Grumman Aerospace. We were under contract to produce flaps, spoilers and ailerons for the F-14 fighter. Having experience with the C-5A Lockheed program made us more cautious when bidding the F-14 project. We entered into negotiations with Grumman and reached a satisfactory agreement.

Grumman in the meantime was trying to renegotiate their F-14 contract with DOD (Department of Defense) because they had been losing money. Senator Cannon of Nevada was Chairman of the DOD Sub-committee that was dealing with this. We were visited by a team from his sub-committee, wanting to discuss our sub-contract and if we were requesting a renegotiation of our contract with Grumman. When they realized that we weren't, then they wanted to know why, and we told them because we were satisfied with our price.

Congressional Hearings were held in Washington, D.C. and the CEO, Jack Anderson and I went to testify. This was a new experience. The government was using us to counter Grumman's request to renegotiate the price. This was a difficult position to be in but we were able to deflect most of the obstacles. The time that we were in Washington was the same time that the "Watergate" break-in occurred. We were staying at the Watergate and knew nothing about what was happening.

NOAA (National Oceanic Atmospheric Administration) was interested in upgrading their C-130 "hurricane hunters" to allow data from flying through a hurricane to be data linked to the ground immediately instead of having to land and transfer tapes and disks to a computer center for analysis. We bid on the program and were successful in winning it. As part of the contract we had to install a new financial and management system that would satisfy new DOD reporting requirements. This was new and there were only a few contactors who had been able to meet these stringent requirements.

LTV in Texas was one company that had passed the requirements. We contacted them and they agreed to assist us in implementing this new system. We would successfully implement the system over the next year. As a result we were one of a handful that was qualified to bid on programs with this requirement.

The NOAA project went on to be a very successful and profitable program.

Although Kaman was originally a helicopter manufacturer for the Navy, there were no new helicopter programs available. Vietnam had ramped up and it didn't appear to be ending any time soon. DOD funding was getting difficult for new programs but there appeared to be an unlimited amount of R & D funding available. This was meant to allow government contractors to keep a minimum engineering base available until funding restraints were lifted.

The Air Force had $5+ million for a project that was considered "questionable." We were having many of our aircraft shot down over the central part of Vietnam and we were having difficulty recovering the pilots. If they could bail out and have the ability to travel 50+ miles to the sea, a rescue could be more successful.

The idea was to have, as part of the seat, a rotary craft that had blades folded along the back of the seat and a small engine under the seat. A parachute would stabilize the seat and then the blades would unfold, cut the parachute shrouds and the pilot would guide it to the sea. We were successful in getting the contract but we were not successful in working out the engineering issues and the project was cancelled.

Another project that we were successful in winning was "LAMPS" (Light Airborne Multi-purpose System). This project was to monitor bad actor submarines by putting sonobuoys in the ocean at strategical locations and as movement went between them information would be data linked to a helicopter that was on station over the area. The helicopter would then transfer that information to the ship for analysis. To test this concept, it was decided by the military that Vietnam would be an ideal test area. The equivalent of sonobuoys would be placed in the jungle and as the Viet Cong traveled between them, data would be data linked to a helicopter on site and then transferred back to base. The movements of the VietCong would be monitored.

This actually worked fairly well and the ship program was given a go ahead.

One problem with the ship program was that the ships had to be modified to handle the helicopters. This was a major project and delayed the implementation of the program for a number of years.

As Kaman Aerospace became more successful, Jack Anderson received permission to look at acquisitions where there might be synergy. We looked at Engstrom Helicopter but that was too small. We also looked at a company called ILC Industries. They were owned by International Latex and consisted of three divisions: ILC Steinthal, a parachute company; ILC Dover, a manufacturer of Space Suits for the astronauts; and ILC Data Device, a manufacturer of data device electronic circuit boards.

ILC appeared to be an interesting opportunity. When Jack presented this to Charley Kaman it was rejected as Kaman was moving into the music industry. Charley had also been a musician in his youth and had invented a round back guitar that we were producing in small quantities in our Moosup plant.

Charley had recently hired Glenn Campbell to endorse the guitar. He had also decided to acquire a number of music distributing companies. The profits from our operation were being used to fund the new Music Division.

Sharon and I had rented the house in Bloomfield for a year and we decided that we needed to look at a more permanent solution.

I saw in the paper that lots were being sold in North Granby, CT. North Granby was less than 10 miles from

Bloomfield. We took a ride to see what was being offered. A farm was being broken up for development and they were selling lots of about 10 to 13 acres. These lots were on top of a hill, in a rural area. We decided to buy a lot and build. There was an ad in the paper by a builder with a design for a house that was very colonial, 4 bedrooms, two levels with a basement and over 2,500 S/F. We looked at the quality of the builders work and were impressed. We decided to move forward with this.

Because of the altitude of where we were going to build, (some 1,600 feet), the home would not have air conditioning. Heat was in the ceiling. Wires were laid in the sheet rock and coated over. This was indirect heat but very affective. We had a large deck installed on the back of the house overlooking the woods and we had a family room with plank floors and a large fireplace.

We wanted a large wooden mantle over the fireplace. The builder asked how large and I said at least 8" square and all the way across the fireplace- at least 10 feet. The builder checked and said that he couldn't find anything that large but that he was going to Vermont and he would look there. When he came back he said he found something that would work and he also found some old barn siding that would go on the walls of the family room. It worked out perfectly and made the room very comfortable.

The house turned out better than expected. We were in the country but close enough to the city that we had the best of all worlds. In all, there would be less than ten homes on the farm property that was being sub-divided.

The summer of our first year in Connecticut we decided to take a vacation in Maine. We found a house for rent on Casco Bay and reserved it. My father and mother indicated that they would like to visit us so I invited them to go with us. What a mistake. We drove to Portland and found the ferry that we were to take. No cars allowed so we parked in the lot. The ferry ride was about an hour and it was an experience for all. Robin was eight, Scott going on seven and Stacy two. This was the vacation from hell. The cottage we had rented was very basic. There was no beach, only a rocky shoreline and not many cottages on the island and no stores. The water was too cold for the children to get in. Everyone was glad when the week ended and we could get back to civilization.

We did visit the LL Bean store before going home.

There was a ski area within 20 minutes of our new house and when winter came we all decided to learn to ski. This worked out fairly well except Scott fell and broke his leg taking lessons and I sprained my ankle. I would have been better if I had broken it. The ski area wasn't far from Winsted, Conn. There was a small hospital there with very good doctors who took care of both of us.

The following year we decided to go to Vermont after Christmas. We went to the Sugarbush resort over the Christmas holidays. We rented a condo on the sloops and had a great time although there wasn't a lot of snow until we were ready to come home.

In the summer one of the folks at the company introduced me to bass fishing. Connecticut is full of small ponds/lakes that are full of bass. We would take a 14 foot jon boat, strap it to the top of our station wagon and go fishing every Thursday evening. We could get to almost everywhere in Connecticut in about an hour. We would leave after work and fish until 10:00 or 11:00 and then head home.

Twin Lakes was in the Northwest corner of the state and we found it had not only bass but trout. It was a little over an hour's drive and became one of our favorite spots to go. On one of our trips, I was fishing with a bass lure and got the hooks of the lure stuck in my thumb. It was going to need medical attention so we decided to stop at the Winstead Hospital on the way home.

Fortunately the Doctor who had treated me for the skiing sprain was on duty. He took a look and said "I think we can save the lure." Surprisingly he did.

In 1971, one of the folks at the office, Don Laurie, and I decided to go bear hunting in Maine. We would go to Stratton, Maine where there was a hunting camp with a guide. Stratton was very close to the Canadian border. We signed up for a week of hunting. The guide used dogs. We would go out at the crack of dawn and travel the dirt roads with a strike dog in a crate at the front of an old milk truck. The rest of the dogs were in the back and we stood in the front. Each day one of us was the main hunter and the other, the backup. Travelling the dirt roads, the strike dog would start to howl if they smelled a bear that had crossed the road. The guide could tell by how they howled if it was fresh or old. If it was new, we would stop and he would release the strike dog. Based upon his barking he would decide whether to release the pack in the back of the truck. Once they were released we would then follow them hoping that they would lead us to a bear that was treed.

The first day that we struck a bear, we went up the hill and down the hill and after about three hours the dogs had treed a bear and her two cubs. Since this was a mother bear and her cups we left her alone and returned to the truck.

The second day it was my turn to be first. We struck a bear soon after we started and chased it up the hill, down the hill, through the blueberry bushes and a swamp and finally treed it. It was an old boar and nasty. We pulled the dogs away from the tree and tried to get the bear down. I shot it first with my rifle and then it fell and I then shot it with my 357 pistol. I understood why the guide had insisted that we have a handgun as well as a rifle. Going through the brush, it was easy to lose your rifle. We gathered all of the dogs and then proceeded to skin the bear and take the meat off the skin. We then tied the skin to a pole to carry out the pelt and meat.

When we got back to camp, we then finished the cleaning of the bear and preserved the skin and the meat.

This was quite the experience. Don wasn't successful in getting a bear but had a great time. Later that evening, we were sitting around outside, when another hunting group came in with a bear strapped to the top of their Cadillac.

They were from New York City and they were dressed like they were on a safari. They were on a guaranteed hunt, meaning that they only paid if they shot a bear. As a result the guide had placed them on a baited stand near the town dump. They had shot a bear and put it on the top of their car and brought it back to camp. The guide suggested that they needed to clean the bear. They said no thanks and went to their cabin. Obviously, they were city hunters.

On our way home we stopped in Groveton, New Hampshire to visit friends of Don. They worked in a manufacturing company and were great hunters. We had dinner with them and they invited us to come deer hunting with them later in the year. Don was surprised because they didn't usually invite any outsiders. We thanked them and took them up on their offer later in the year.

When I got home I made arrangements to have the bear skin made into a rug. We had salted it down in Maine and I ended up shipping it to a tannery in California. There were no tannery facilities on the east coast. We cut the meat up and froze it. We would eat the meat later that year.

I also hunted deer with a bow and arrow in the Barkhamsted Forrest of Connecticut. I was never able to kill one but I saw a number and had a great time getting into the forest. You couldn't hunt with a rifle on state land in Conn.

Sharon took Robin and Scott to horseback riding lessons just across the state line in Mass. Scott fell off shortly after starting and decided that this wasn't for him. Robin continued and the lessons have led to over 50 years of horses in her life, continuing to this day.

We took one Saturday and decided that we were going to try to touch most of the New England states in one day. We drove North through Massachusetts into Vermont, turned east and entered New Hampshire then turned south to Rhode Island and then back home in Connecticut. We touched all but Maine in that journey.

Boston was going to have an NFL football team and they were going to play in Foxborough, Mass. This was about 2 hours from our home. Season tickets were available at a reasonable price so I bought 4 season tickets. Stacy was still only 2 so she didn't need a ticket. We had good seats but the language of the fans was terrible and it finally got so bad that we gave our seats up after a year.

In mid- 1971, Jack Anderson was unexpectedly fired. No one knew why and this caused quite an upheaval. I was called into the office of the Senior VP of Finance of the Corporation and told that I would be reporting to him for the time being. We never had a good relationship and I wasn't sure how this was going to work. I had a very honest discussion about our relationship and it was decided that we would give it a few weeks to see how it would work.

After a few weeks it was obvious that this wasn't going to work. It was decided that I would leave and an agreement was reached to keep me on the payroll for 6 months as a severance arrangement. I was now 33 years old with a wife and 3 children. I was one of the early mobile corporate executives. You advanced by moving to a new company. I contacted a number of executive search firms and I also met with Jack Anderson for his counsel. I asked him what had happened and he said that Charlie Kaman didn't want to reinvest in the Aerospace industry but that he wanted to expand the music business and the bearing business. He planned to use the profits of the aerospace operation for that expansion and that he and Jack couldn't see eye to eye. Jack was weighing a number of opportunities and would be making a decision soon as to what he planned to do.

I had a number of interviews with government contracting companies but at 33 and with the senior positions that I had held, companies were reluctant to consider me as it was still an old boys' network. I was either too young or too experienced.

Jack ended up taking the position of C.E.O. at ILC Industries in Wilmington, DE. This was a company that we had looked at purchasing but Kaman turned the opportunity down. ILC Industries was a public company but most of the stock was owned by International Latex Corporation.

ILC Industries consisted of three subsidiaries: ILC Steinthal, ILC Data Device and ILC Dover. ILC Dover was based in Dover Delaware and their product was the Space Suits for the Apollo astronauts. ILC Data Device was based in Hicksted Long Island and produced thick and thin film circuit boards. ILC Steinthal was in Westchester County, New York but their manufacturing facility was in Roxboro, NC, twenty miles north of Durham.

Jack contacted me in late 1971 and wanted to know if I was interested in joining him at ILC Industries. This was a turn- around situation and he needed help. He offered me the position of Executive Vice President of Operations. I would be responsible for operations instead of finance. Sharon and I discussed this and she said that it was my decision. What a trooper. I decided that this was an opportunity that was too good to turn down. It was a change to be involved in the day to day operations of a multi- faceted company. I told Jack that I would join him.

He said that I would be based at Wilmington, DE. for the time being but that he wanted to see how everything played out before deciding whether that would be headquarters. He had a corporate apartment and indicated that I could stay there during the week. I would be commuting, as was he, but we would also be spending time at each of the operations.

I would be away from home during the week but home on week-ends. Again, Sharon had her hands full with a 4 year old, a ten year old and an 8 year old. As always she picked up the slack and allowed me to follow my heart.

I started in January 1972 and I visited each operation and reviewed their operating plans. It was obvious that this had been a company without a rudder for a while. Organization and structure was missing. The most serious issues seemed to be at ILC Steinthal. Two brothers, Martin and Augie Steinthal, had taken over the company that their father had started. Their manufacturing operation had been in Brooklyn NY but in the early 1950's they had moved to Roxboro, NC. for the lower labor rates. They kept their headquarters in New Rochelle, NY. They had made a good life from the business of making parachutes for the military. They were primarily a cut and sew business.

They had sold the company in the early 1960's but then bought it back within a year for a fraction of what they had sold it for and then proceeded to sell it again to ILC Industries. They were still 1950 style managers and I found them to be wonderful individuals but they had retired in place. This was the biggest problem that we had, so Jack said that he wanted me to spend the next few months analyzing all aspects of the operation.

I started at the corporate office for Steinthal. They had a small staff but all estimating was done in New Rochelle. A small engineering staff was also based in New Rochelle. The sons of both brothers were also involved in the business but it was difficult to determine what they did. Augie was involved in the plant operations in North Carolina and Martin was the face of the business. Martin belonged to the Metropolitan Club in New York City, and also the Winged Foot Country Club in Westchester County. Augie was a member of the Westchester County Country Club.

I traveled to North Carolina to see the operations. There was a plant manager, an industrial engineering department, a mechanics group and a small purchasing operation and about 350 sewing machine operators.

As I continued my due diligence, I found that I was spending a few days in New Rochelle and the balance of the week in North Carolina. The purpose was to try to determine why this operation had been losing money for some time and was still losing money.

The facility seemed to be busy. As I talked with the staff the first thing that came to light was that there was little or no direction from New Rochelle. There was little or no communication and pricing decisions were being made without input from North Carolina.

I also found that every year, around September/October, almost 1/3 of the manufacturing facility had to be vacated because the owner of the building was a tobacco farmer and that part of the facility was used for tobacco sales. This is when the local tobacco farmers bring their cured tobacco in to warehouses and spread their tobacco out on the floor in sheets and tobacco auctions are held with tobacco companies sending their buyers in to purchase it. This process was between two to three months and disrupted the manufacturing process.

In my review of the contracts, I found that they were continually running out of hardware for the parachutes and having to reorder. This was not only costly but time consuming, since most hardware was coming from England. As I continued my review I found that there was no inventory control and when parts were received there was no count.

Further inspection determined that the receiving department had employees doing this work that had difficulty with reading and writing and therefore just accepted whatever came in. Steinthal was making parachutes for the F-111 aircraft pilot escape capsule, personnel parachutes, cargo parachutes and miscellaneous parachutes for bombs.

The biggest problem appeared to be the bidding process. The concept of marginal pricing is fine providing all of the assumptions remain true. On pricing a new contract, the estimators would look at what business was in house and how much overhead was priced into the contracts and then compare this to the total overhead estimated to be incurred for the year. When they determined that all overhead was covered they would then price the overhead for a new contract at a reduced amount.

The concept works if all your assumptions hold true. However, in their case they had delays because of needing more materials. The disruption due to giving up space for tobacco was an issue and the bottom line was that none of the assumptions held true and therefore they continued to lose more money. Marginal pricing was a folly.

After spending a number of months reviewing everything I put together a report that recommended that we close the New Rochelle Office and move all operations to North Carolina. Martin and Augie and their sons were not necessary going forward and exit packages needed to be established for them. A search should begin for a new President and a new lease needed to be executed that kept the company from halting production in September and October from 1/3 of the space.

This was a major change for their operations but necessary if the company had a change to reverse their losses.

The report was reviewed by Jack and it was decided that we would move forward with my recommendations.

This was somewhat traumatic for the Steinthals, but they realized that it was necessary. A transition was worked out that was difficult but necessary.

The next order of business was to transition the corporate office to North Carolina and then begin a search for a new President.

After a search for a few months, we arrived at a candidate that we felt would be able to move the company forward. He was a seasoned parachute engineer and well respected in the field. He was from California. He accepted and moved east. We completed the move and then augmented our staff with those vacancies that were a result of the move.

I was given the assignment of managing the transition and also of managing the aftermath.

In addition to parachutes, Steinthal had also entered into producing recreational tents for Kamart. This was a fairly sizeable business but the business model put most of the risk unto Steinthal.

Kamart had two manufacturers, one for west of the Mississippi and one for east. The basis was to minimize transportation costs. Each year you presented a series of tents and prices to the buyer at Kamart and he would decide what models were going to be sold. They would then select from both submittals and new prices had to be negotiated based upon the estimated volume of each by Kamart. You did not get paid until 30 days after delivery and inventory was your risk. If they did not take all of the tents that they projected, they said that they would try to take them first the following year. However there was no guarantee.

It was up to you to determine how many and of what type to produce. If you guessed right then all was well, but if not then a problem could develop. The annual buy was approximately $1 to 2 Million per year.

Steinthal had also decided to produce their own line of tents under their own label, "North Star." The problem was that they had no marketing plan. It was decided that we would continue with this line of business but we needed to develop a marketing plan and staff.

We hired a marketing director from Coleman Industries, a camping and outdoor company.

A business plan was developed, that if executed could provide for the turn around that Steinthal needed. I also brought in Doug Stover from Kaman to be the Controller. I needed to shore up the financial department.

Toward the end of 1972 it was obvious that the program at Steinthal was not proceeding as we had anticipated. The new President was indecisive and never fully took control of the operation. It was obvious that we needed to cut our losses. As we discussed this at the corporate office, Jack suggested that I should move to North Carolina and take over the operation as President on a full time basis.

After some soul searching and discussions with Sharon it was decided that this was a high risk opportunity but again it was up to me. I decided to accept the job and the risk that went with it. We made the physical move after school was out in May/June 1973. I had found an older home on 13+ acres with an old barn and equipment shed outside of Roxboro and bought it. This was a new adventure for all.

I decided that we needed to live in the community of Roxboro and not Durham where almost all of the managers lived. If I was going to be able to turn this company around, I needed to be involved in the community.

In addition to moving the normal household goods, we had a sailboat to move. During one of my stays in New York, in early 1972, I went to the New York Boat Show and was captivated by the sailboats. I had never sailed but I thought this for be a great activity for the family. Bayreuther Boat Company of Niantic, CT. had a display with a 23 foot O'Day sailboat on display. No one was at their booth so I took down their telephone number and called on Monday morning.

I reached one of the brothers, Warren, and told him I was thinking about sailing and I asked what the 23 foot O'Day price was. He told me $9,500. I told him that I would buy it if they would give us sailing lessons and if we could keep it at his facility. He said that wasn't an issue but he would hold it until I had a chance to check it out. I said fine, we would be down the following Saturday.

We did go down the next Saturday and reached an arrangement and purchased the boat. They gave us lessons and I also enrolled for a class in sailing at the Annapolis Sailing School. I followed that up with a class in Coastal Navigation and then I took a class in racing. We spent the summer week-ends sailing and soon found that the boat was too small for our family of 5.

They also represented other boat manufacturers including Grampian. Grampian was a manufacturer of sailboats in Ontario, Canada. They had one called the "Grampian 30." It was a cruising machine.

On one of our day sails, we were returning to the dock and Warren was there to meet us. He said "I just sold your boat." By the end of the day we would be the proud owners of a new Grampian 30 sailboat. However, we would need to wait for a month or so because it was on order.

When it did arrive, we had it outfitted and we were ready to go. We spent the summer sailing Long Island Sound. Our favorite locations included Shelter Island, Block Island and Mystic Seaport.

When it came time to relocate, we decided to have the sailboat hauled to Edenton, N.C. where Grampian had another facility. We quickly learned that the sailing Capital of North Carolina was Oriental so we quickly made arrangements to relocate the boat there. We moved it ourselves. Edenton is on the Western end of Albemarle Sound. We needed to go east and then turn into the Alligator River and follow that to Belhaven and then into Pamlico Sound and finally end up at Oriental. The day we left it was 95 degrees, no wind, 3 children and a dog.

When we reached the Alligator River there was a terrific storm. We tied up to a channel marker and rode it out. We finally made it to Oriental, two days later.

This was a great location but it was 4 hours from Roxboro and in Connecticut we were only an hour from the boat. We realized that this wasn't going to work and after trying to charter it and having issues we decided to sell the boat and stay closer to home.

As we started to implement a marketing program for our tent program, I was introduced to a tent designer by the name of Bill Moss. He had developed some innovative tents and was looking for a manufacturer. That led me to Alain Clenet. Alain was also a designer who had worked for Bill Moss but now was starting his own design company in California and needed a manufacturer. His product was a cover for the rear of a pickup truck. It was featured on Bill Hickey's trucks that were designed for the Rockford Files TV series featuring

Jim Gardner. Alain was an engineer from France where his family was involved in Formula 1 racing.

We eventually entered into arrangements with both Bill Moss and Alain Clenet. Bill Moss's tents were innovative and an incorporated a new concept, lighter and smaller. The covers were to become also an innovative product. General Motors was to purchase over a thousand. I went to GM with Alain Clenet. I must say quite an experience. However I was also surprised that they were not as well organized as I expected, coming from the aerospace industry.

We also were asked to consider manufacturing a line of expanded vinyl travel accessories for another company. As we looked at the opportunity, the marketing manager wanted to know if we wanted to purchase the business as it didn't fit into the long term plan of his company.

It was decided that we would enter into discussions and review the opportunity. This was a commercial cut and sew operation and we would need a marketing program here also. After a number of discussions I could see that they just wanted to get rid of the business and we agreed to take it and pay them a royalty for the first year.

With the new lines of business we had increased our manpower to over 700 employees. The local community college assisted by holding training programs for sewers. We also leased a 25,000 sf building for inventory and finished goods from a local farmer for $2.50 per sf

We renegotiated the lease on our current facility and therefore would no longer have to relocate each year. We did have to convert our sprinkler system from a dry to wet system and that entailed installing new pumps at a cost of $10,000.

At this time we needed to expand our workforce even more. I said to the staff, "why not establish a second shift." Jim Barker our head industrial engineer said that it would not work. I kept asking him why it wouldn't work but all he would say is that it would not work. I said well let's try it.

He was right. It didn't work, but he could not explain why? The problem was that the sewing machine is an individual work station with tensions set for a specific user. By trying a second shift, the second shift employee would have to change the tensions to suit themselves.

The next morning the machine would have to be changed again and machines were breaking down and the mechanics could not keep up with the issues.

I quickly saw the issues and stopped that experiment.

We were paying the minimum wage of $1.65 per hour plus an incentive based upon piece counts. The productivity was terrible. I decided to raise the minimum to $1.75 and change the standards for piece work. The standards had been set so that they were not attainable and therefore we had a huge morale issue. By changing the standards and raising the minimum wage, morale soared and productivity increased exponentially. As a result, we were able to resolve production issues associated with the increased opportunities.

We decided to make Friday's, "Casual Friday." This meant that all employees could wear casual clothes on Friday. This also helped in increasing productivity because, in the summer months, most employees left for the beach or had other activities planned after work. This allowed them the opportunity of leaving immediately after work.

Staffing had to be increased so I hired an experienced cut and sew HR manager, John Lancaster. John was instrumental in changing many processes that had handicapped our work force in the past.

We were also asked to consider making a line of expanded vinyl travel accessories for another company. We made samples and thought that this could be an interesting commercial opportunity. The company was a distributor of medical devices and this product line didn't fit their business model. I was given approval to see if they would sell the product to us. For less than $10,000, we now had another product line.

We decided to move the expanded vinyl line into tennis accessories. I had a manufacturing consultant, Jim Teat, from Charlotte, NC. helping me resolve various manufacturing issues. Jim's son was working for Donald Dell, a sports agent who had a number of tennis players under contract. A meeting was arraigned with Donald. He and I agreed to meet at The U.S. Open Tennis tournament in Forest Hills, New York.

Donald introduced me to a number of tennis players. He indicated that he thought Tom Gorman might be right person for what we wanted to do. Tom had just signed an endorsement with a company making tennis clothes. We could ride on their coattails. After some discussion, we agreed and the cost to us was $10,000 plus a small royalty.

Our next step was to put a catalog together of the products with Tom. This would be the major marketing piece.

We decided to present our new line at the sporting goods association trade show in Houston. We also decided to show our commercial line of tents at that show. There were two trade sporting goods shows a year, Houston and Chicago.

As we were moving more and more into commercial product lines, inventory was now an issue. We needed funds in order to build up inventory. This was more demanding than the government parachutes but also could be more profitable.

We received an inquiry from Steve Snyder, the owner and designer of a sports parachuting company, to produce a commercial sky diving parachute that he had a patent on. We decided to enter into an agreement with Steve and our first order was for 200 parachutes.

We started to deliver the order to Steve but within weeks we received inquiries stating that these parachutes did not fly straight but that they had a turn in them. We had about 50 chutes that had not been delivered so I made the decision that we would go to the local airport, hire some skydivers and test each of the chutes.

Upon doing that, we found that they all had a turn in them. We stopped production until we could determine what was wrong.

We revisited the manufacturing floor and followed a parachute from beginning to end. We found that one sewer was taking an extra fold before sewing her panel and as a result this caused the chute to turn.

We proceeded to fix the chutes and recalled all that had been delivered.

We now had over 700 employees and in addition to the government product lines of personnel, cargo and flare parachutes, we had commercial lines for Kamart Tents, Northstar Tents, truck covers, skydiving chutes, and expanded vinyl accessories.

Eventually we also moved into silk screening t- shirts and other items as well as artic tents for the military.

Within a year we had added significantly to the volume of ILC Steinthal but at the cost of increased inventory. ILC Dover was having issues with their core business as there was a lull in spacesuits. At ILC Data Device there were challenges with the new thick and thin film electronic devices. At the same time, the ILC Corporate shareholder decided that they did not want to be the banker for ILC Industries any longer.

In early 1975, I was told that the owners of ILC wanted to close the Steinthal operation. I was asked to put together a "going out of business" plan. How could we close the operation with the least amount of disruption? This was a difficult assignment. I had taken the job knowing that it was a turn- around situation. I had done everything that was necessary to make that happen and now I was asked to close it down. They were moving the ILC Industries corporate office to New York City and they wanted me to come back to the corporate office.

After a great deal of soul searching and discussion with the family, I decided that I couldn't do it. I prepared the plan but I said that I could not in good consciousness execute it.

Moving to Roxboro and getting involved in local community activities had changed me. I felt like I finally found my home. My family felt the same way. I wasn't prepared to move again.

An agreement was reached that I would leave the company but that they would continue paying me for a year. I had no idea what I was going to do but I knew it was time to get off this roller coaster when my children said, "do we have to move again?"

Robin was now 13, Scott 11 and Stacy 7.

I had gotten to know most of the business owners in Roxboro and I decided that I would try to see if I could purchase the Roxboro operation.

After getting local support and talking to Erskine Bowles, the son of the Secretary of State for North Carolina, I made an offer to Jack Anderson that I felt was reasonable but it was turned down. They had changed their mine and did not want to sell. They were prepared to run the current business out and then close the company down. This made no sense, but it was obvious that I was not in good standing with them since I would not close the business down and move to New York. I finally gave up trying to work something out and decided it was time to determine my next step.

I already had a real estate broker's license from Connecticut and wondered whether this might be a viable move. I had taken a real estate course at the University of Hartford while working at Kaman. I took and passed the Brokers exam in Connecticut. I was an investor in a time-share real estate investment in Spain along with three other Kaman executives. One of the individuals was married to a woman from Switzerland and she had contacts in Europe that were developing a time share community on the Costa Blanca of Spain. We were able to acquire the American marketing rights but one of us had to have a Real Estate Brokers License.

The venture wasn't successful because this was the beginning of time-sharing and American's had difficulty understanding how one could own one twelfth of a home. This wasn't a successful venture but it had piqued my interest in real estate as an investment.

I applied for reciprocity with North Carolina. That was granted and I decided to review the possibilities of starting a real estate brokerage company. We were 20 miles North of Durham and Hyco Lake set a few miles north of Roxboro.

Hyco was a Carolina Power & Light lake that was established in the 1960's as a power generating facility, coal fired. The lake was to act as a cooling facility. The lake was large, with 120 miles of shoreline. There were many week-end homes on the lake but the two local real estate firms were not that interested in selling lake property.

After reviewing the real estate market in Durham and Roxboro I decided to establish a brokerage operation in Durham with emphasis on Hyco Lake property as well as residential homes in Durham. There was only one major real estate firm in Durham and it was not very creative. I also applied to the Graduate Realtors Institute (GRI) at the University of North Carolina-Chapel Hill. It was the oldest in the nation and upon completion of the two year course (in the summer) you would receive the designation GRI.

Bert Engstrom, who was my Director of Marketing at Steinthal, left the company at the same time that I did. I encouraged Bert to take a real estate course and get his real estate license. He did and he then joined me in the Durham office. Bert was in charge of the Durham office while I tried to develop the market for Hyco Lake property. My attorney in Roxboro, Mike Carden, lived at the lake and handled all of our closings.

Mike saw that the Hyco Lake market was developing into a very nice business and asked me to consider a partnership to develop a 120 acre farm that one of his clients owned and had Hyco Lake access.

The land was at the eastern end of Hyco. We worked out an arrangement with the seller where we would pay him a certain amount from each lot sale. I had two customers from the Northern Virginia area that were looking for lake property so I showed them the land from a boat. They were both interested and decided that they wanted to be in "Whetstone."

They put a deposit on lots that were not surveyed yet and for which there was no road access yet. We proceeded to sign a purchase agreement for the 120 acres and used the down-payment from the two purchasers for our down-payment. The purchase price amounted to $240,000.

John Lancaster, my Director of HR at Steinthal, had introduced me to his brother in law, Bill Bowling. Bill was an architect out of Roanoke, VA. Bill had been Chief of Design at Hayes, Seay, Mattern and Mattern, a large regional architectural firm based in Roanoke, VA, but had left and was starting his own firm. I contacted Bill and asked him to meet with us to discuss a lake development. Bill came to Roxboro and reviewed our plan.

We wanted to have an upscale development with underground electricity to all of the lots. This would insure that the lots would sell at a premium price, $10,000 to $20,000. As we reviewed the waterfront, it appeared that we would only be able to get about 12 to 14 waterfront lots, ranging from 1 to 3 acres each. We engaged Bill to develop a masterplan and proceeded to have the property surveyed.

The next step was to put roads in and work out an arrangement with Carolina and Power to put the electric underground. The roads were not an issue but it took over 6 months to get CP&L to agree to put the electric underground. Total cost $3,000. Once that was accomplished, we had a large custom wood carved sign made for the entrance saying "Whetstone." We were now ready to put a sales effort on for the remaining waterfront lots. Our plan was to sell out in 4 years. However, our first sale, after the sale to the two Northern Virginia owners, was to the owner of the Budweiser distributorship in Durham, N.C. He proceeded to buy the point lot for $25,000 and build a magnificent vacation home. Other buyers from the Durham area came and within 18 months we had sold all the waterfront lots and paid off the balance on the property.

We still had almost 100 acres of land that wasn't waterfront to sell. Some of our purchasers were Doctor's at Duke's Medical Facility in Durham and Professors at Duke. We were about 45 minutes away from Duke and this was just inside the time allowed for the Doctor's to get to Duke if there was an emergency.

Our real estate business was becoming self-sufficient and I decided to move the operation to Roxboro and concentrate on developing the market there. I had taken in a partner from a large Durham real estate firm but he wasn't holding up his end so I decided there was no need to continue with him.

Bert decided to move back to California, where he and June had moved from, and the timing made it convenient. I was asked to consider teaching Real Estate 101 at the local Piedmont Community College. I always wanted to teach and I decided to give it a try. In order to be licensed in North Carolina you had to take a real estate course and then pass a state wide exam.

My wife, Sharon, was one of my first students. She proceeded to pass the Broker's exam and became a member of the firm. Over the next few years we expanded and suddenly I had 5 sales agents. We became the largest firm in the area. We also bought two convenience stores with gas pumps and developed a Party Store selling beer and wine and party accessories. We purchased over 10 rental properties and started to do some building at the Lake with one of the local builders that we had started a relationship.

I developed a banking relationship with a local bank whose manager was John Jennette. We were members of the local Episcopal Church (we were Lutheran but there was no Lutheran Church in Roxboro). John's family was also.

Robin continued with her horseback riding by taking lessons with Gen Wiseman in Danville, VA., about 35 minutes away. Scott became interested in the Boy Scouts and Stacy took dancing lessons. We became imbedded in the local community and I felt that this was home more than anywhere that we had ever lived. Our friends included the leaders in the community. I became involved in the Boy Scouts and ended up as the Hycotee District Chairman. Sharon became the leader of the Roxboro Girl Scouts Cookie Campaign.

Along the way John Jennette, the Bank manager, called me and said that he and one other were going hiking along the Appalachian Trial in Western North Carolina and they would like for me to join them. I hadn't been camping since Army Basic Training but decided that I better go as this was a "Command Performance" coming from my banker. I borrowed all the camping gear from my son, Scott. We left one Thursday afternoon to drive to the Smoky Mountains, between North Carolina and Tennessee. We were to meet the other member there and then proceed to hike about 50 miles in three days.

We arrived late in the afternoon and parked the cars in a parking area and started out on a macadam road that was inclining upward at a slight angle. I thought that this wasn't bad but then the road suddenly ended. It appeared that the land in front of us went straight up. John said that we would camp for the night at the top. The land was so steep that we had to use small trees to grab onto to help get up the hill. I found out later that we were going up in elevation about two thousand feet. It started to rain and then after a few hours we finally reached the top in the dark.

We found a level area and pitched our tents. We were soaked, tired and hungry and no one was up to try cooking. We just wanted to get out of the wet clothes and get some sleep.

The next morning I woke to the sound of mooing. I looked out the tent and found that we were surrounded by a herd of cows. We were in a farmer's cow field. We got all of our things together and decided to move on down the ridge before we had breakfast. We were on a high ridge on the Appalachian Trial. The views were amazing. As we moved down the ridge I saw an old vehicle coming across a field and the passengers were hooping and hollering. It was almost like a scene out of "Deliverance." We weren't sure what to make of this but we later found that they were "ramp" hunting. We continued until we found a quiet place and had breakfast. After breakfast, we hiked until dusk and make camp for the evening. The next morning we hiked the trial again until we reached a main road. We were able to catch a ride to where we had parked our cars. Finally, the trip was over. I had to admit that it was fun but not something that I wanted to do again.

Roxboro 1975 - Front: Stacy, Sharon, Scott & Robin-Rear -Jess

Chapter Sixteen

In the fall, John called me again and said that they were going to go to LeConte Lodge in the Smokies. I said thanks but I couldn't make it. John said I had to come. This was going to be an easy trip as we would be just hiking up to the Lodge, staying the night and returning the next day. I thought ok, one more time. We got to the Smokies, an 8 hour trip, parked and got our gear and started up the mountain. LeConte Lodge was managed by the Park Service and was about 5 miles up the Mountain. It was September and a little chilly but not bad. It was an easy hike and at the top we came to the lodge. There was a main building that served as the headquarters and the mess hall and then there were a number of smaller buildings that were bunk houses, four bunks to a building. They were bunk beds and nothing else.

There was an outhouse but signs indicated that one should not go out at night because of the bears. I asked about all the marks on the door of the bunkhouses and was told that they were bear marks.

There were no roads in to this Lodge and it was really pretty basic. All supplies had to come in by pack horse. The food was basic and made mostly from trial packs that you would add water to. Not what I was expecting when I was told we were going to a Lodge.

The next morning we ate breakfast and then started to hike the trial. We were going to hike the trial for the day, camp and then head back to where we had parked the cars. We found that it had snowed the night before and it was getting really cold. We hiked the trial until we came to a shelter. In front of the shelter, which was a lean to, was a chain link fence with only a small area to squeeze through to the shelter. This was a bear fence so that you were protected if a bear came. Your food was to be hauled up by a rope into a tree outside. We stayed the night and the next morning headed back to the car as it was getting really cold.

It was an experience but I said that was the end of my camping experience with John. When the next call came I had many excuses why I couldn't make it.

In June of 1980, our real estate business was now over five years old and developing nicely. However, I was getting bored. Robin was getting ready to graduate from high school.

Scott was two years behind and Stacy was going on 12 years of age. I wondered whether I could make the transition back to a corporate environment. I had been a drop out for over 5 years and I was going on 42. I decided to test the water. I answered an ad in the Wall Street Journal for Arvin Industries. They were located in Columbus, Indiana. I received a call and was invited to Columbus to meet with the President. They were looking for a VP of Finance. Arvin was primarily an auto parts manufacturer. I had a good meeting but I realized that there was an issue. I was still fairly young but I had experience that was far more than my age. They were concerned that I might become bored.

However, that trip told me that I needed to do something other than Real Estate for the rest of my life. It was obvious that transitioning back was going to be more difficult than I expected.

I saw another ad in the Wall Street Journal where The Defense Systems Management College (DSMC) at Fort Belvoir was looking for a Professor of Financial Management. DSMC was DOD's College for Program Managers of Government Programs. Also, they took some folks from DOD Contractors as students.

This was an appointed position and was for a period of 3 years. On a lark I decided to apply. I received a call and was asked to come to Fort Belvoir for an interview and also to make a presentation on any issue of finance that I considered important.

I thought, why not. I prepared a presentation on fixed assets and depreciation and went to my interview. I first met with Dr. Ben Rush, Dean of the School, and then I met with most of the faculty where I gave a presentation. After that I met with the Commandant of the School, General Thurman. General Thurman had been the B-1 Program Manager after having been a pilot in the Air Force.

I didn't think much of this interview but it was interesting. The position was a GS- 14 and a teaching position, something I always thought I would be interested in. It was November 1980. Most of the faculty were military, but there was a number of civilian positions. Most had Doctorates or at least Masters Degrees.

I was a C.P.A. and had excellent experience with Defense Contractors and that was my difference. It wasn't long before I received a call from Dr. Rush and told that they wanted me to join their faculty but that there was a freeze on all positions until after the New Year. If I was interested they would try to work it out. After talking with Sharon, we decided to take a chance. I told them I was interested. I always wanted to get an

M.B.A. and they said that the government would pay for that.

Regan was elected President and the hold on hiring was released. I was officially offered the position. We had a number of decisions to make. What to do about the real estate business, Whetstone and moving? We decided we would not move but that I would commute and find a room in Northern VA. I would come home on weekends. This was a transitional move and hopefully it would allow me to transition back into industry.

I reached an arrangement with one of the real estate employees to take over the business and I sold my interest in Whetstone to my Attorney. Sharon would continue to sell real estate for the firm.

I made arrangements to stay with my Aunt Doris in Springfield until I could find a room, etc.

All was in order, and in early 1981 I started a new page in my book. I found a room in a private home in Alexandria and learned that Tom Daschle, Congressman from South Dakota was in the room next door. He was going through a divorce and was living there also. He was hardly ever there when I was. I remember the one thing that he said about being a Congressman, when you get elected, the next day you start running again, as the term is only 2 years. What a life.

For the next 2 ½ years I commuted from Roxboro to Fort Belvoir and back weekly.

I applied to the M.B.A. program at American University and George Washington University and was admitted to both. I selected GW as I wanted to experience a different school from my undergraduate one. I needed 30 hours of credit for my M.B.A. as I had 30 hours of graduate study in my undergraduate work that would transfer.

This period of time was especially satisfactory as I was doing something that would help others and I was getting an advanced degree paid for by the government.

I made some excellent contacts with peers in the Military as well as civilian life. George (Tony) Perino was an Lt.Col. in the Army and Dr. Jay Billings was a civilian. Both became long-term friends. Most of the students were extremely smart, had advanced degrees and were on the fast track for advancement in their respective services. It was a very rewarding time.

In early 1983, I felt that I needed to reconsider whether I should try to transition back to a corporate position. I was almost finished with my M.B.A. and the travel was becoming difficult with the family. Stacy was getting ready to enter high school and Scott was graduating from High School and Robin was at UNC-Chapel Hill with only a year to go.

I saw an ad for a Sr.VP of Administration for a defense contractor in Norfolk, VA. and I decided to answer it. Surprising, I received a call and was asked to come to Norfolk for an interview. The Company, S.M.A. (Systems Management American) was a minority contractor owned by Herman Valentine. It had been awarded a significant contract with the Navy to install ruggedized computers on board Navy Ships. I went to Norfolk and met with Herman and his Senior Management team. I was impressed with what they had accomplished but now they were entering into another phase of government contracting and needed more experienced individuals to take it to the next level. Herman was also into show horses and had a farm between VA. Beach & Norfolk. We met at his farm and I spent the day with his staff. I was uncertain as to whether this was a good fit but there was something interesting about this position.

I went back to my teaching position at DSMC and within a week I had a call offering me the position at a significant increase in salary over my DSMC salary. After conferring with Sharon, we decided that it was worth the chance and so I accepted the offer. It was late summer of 1983, so we decided to move before school started. We put our house in Roxboro on the market and made arrangements to move.

I found a house to rent in Virginia Beach, one block from the beach on 66th Street. I thought this would be a new experience. My Father had recently passed away and my Mother was alone in Clearfield. I suggested that she was welcome to come and live with us as I felt an obligation to take care of her. She decided to do that and we were now a three generation family.

As I settled into my new position, it was obvious that I needed to augment the financial staff. I called Tony Perino, who had worked with me at DSMC and was now retired from the military, to see if he might be interested in transitioning to the business world. Tony was a retired Lt.Col. who had spent his entire career in the Army as a Ranger and then at DSMC. Tony agreed that it was time for him to put to use his business background and agreed to become my Controller.

Herman had made an offer to Alan Mandel, a recently retired Navy Captain and Contracts Specialist to come aboard as Director of Contracts. I met with Alan and he agreed to take the position. I had my nucleus with Tony and Alan.

As we built a staff and improved the accounting system it was obvious that I would be involved in all aspects of the company. Early on in this new position I was called into Herman's office and told that there was interest in our SNAP (Shipboard Non-tactical Automatic Data Process) system by the Spanish Navy. There was an engineering team in England that could be prepared to go to Madrid to meet the Harris Corporation team that was dealing with the Spanish Navy. I needed to head this team up and I needed to leave the next day and go to England and then take the team to Madrid. After that, Alan Mandel and myself needed to go to Glasgow, Scotland and meet with the Scottish Development Corporation, concerning Artificial Intelligence (AI) and the possibility of a joint venture with the University of Edinburg.

The engineering team that was in England was reviewing a system that was used at Metros for entering and exiting a transportation system. I made arrangements to meet them at their hotel outside of London. When I went to the Norfolk airport I found a significant delay because a plane landing at Norfolk's International Airport had its wheels give out on landing and had stalled everything. I was scheduled to fly to JFK in New York and then catch a flight from there to London.

After reviewing various options, the only way to make my meetings in London was to take the next available flight to LaGuardia in New York, take a taxi to JFK and take the British SST to London. The SST's schedule was 3 ½ hours instead of the normal 6 1/2 hours.

I made the flight, raced in a taxi to JFK and just made the flight to London. At 10:30 P.M. London time we landed at Heathrow. The SST flight ended up being 3 hours and ten minutes. There were 100 seats but they were not much larger than economy seats in a normal aircraft. We flew at 1590 mph. It was an experience.

I made the meetings the next day and then caught a flight to Madrid where we meet with the Spanish Navy. After that meeting, Alan and I flew to Glasgow via London to meet with the Scottish Development Organization. It was an interesting meeting but the company decided not to pursue a research facility in Scotland in AI.

Upon returning home, I had a discussion with my Mother about where I had been. She said that my Great Grandfather Boyle was from Glasgow. She proceeded to bring out various writings that had his address and much more about him, including his time in Scotland. He apparently had been born and raised in Ireland, immigrated to Glasgow during the potato famine in Ireland. He became a minister, married a Scottish woman and then came to America. He apparently traveled back and forth often and was buried in Scotland upon his death. What little we know!

As we ramped up production for the SNAP project, we began getting inquiries from other military services for a ruggedized personal computer. My responsibilities took on more of a COO's role. I had finance, legal, administration and marketing.

The Marine Corps had an interest in our systems and I was selected to take a team to Hawaii to meet with the Joint Command there and then to San Diego to meet with the Marine Corps there. I thought Sharon needed a break so I suggested that she come with me. We could visit the "Big Island" before we went to San Diego. She was reluctant but it was finally agreed that she would join me.

We stayed on Ohau during the week and when I finished my meetings on Friday we flew to the "Big Island" for the week-end. It was great being able to finally spend some time alone, even though we both got so sun burned that we had a hard time putting our clothes on to fly back to San Diego. Once in San Diego, Sharon flew home and I continued with our meetings.

The Air Force had also expressed interest and I later went to San Antonio to meet with the Command there.

We had reached our production targets and were meeting our financial targets when we started to get some interest from investment banks about going public. We meet with a number of investment banks and their analysts. We were also visited by Michael Milken from Drexel Burnham.

Drexel Burnham was extremely interested in taking us public and it appeared that a deal was close when Herman Valentine decided not to pursue going public. This made no sense but later I realized why.

Herman and two of the company's senior managers were being investigated by the government for fraud and kickbacks. This investigation went on for a few years and handicapped the company's operation. In 1987 all the senior officers had been served subpoenas. All ended up obtaining outside counsel, paid for by the company. My attorney was with a large Washington, D.C. based law firm and had been a prosecutor in the Department of Justice, Southern District of NY under Gulliani before leaving to go into private practice.

He would not allow me to meet with the government's lawyers until they granted me immunity. I had no knowledge of the kickbacks, etc. I met a number of times with the government but had very little to tell them.

Sometime in late 1986 or 1987 I had met with Anthony (Tony) Welters. Tony had been interviewed by Herman as a possible individual to run a potential acquisition. Herman's banker, John Gibson, had attempted to get Herman to purchase a company called

American Coastal Industries (ACI). It was based in Chesapeake, VA. and was owned by Stuart and Clifford Perlman. It was in the business of renovating transit cars for the New Jersey Commuter Railroad.

The Perlman's were former owners of Lum's Restaurant and subsequently Caesar's Palace in Las Vegas.

When the Perlman's decided to expand their Casino operation into New Jersey, the were not able to get a gambling license until they relinquished control of Caesar's because it was said that they were too close to members of the mafia. They subsequently sold their interest in Caesar's and started to develop real estate in New Jersey. They also purchased the facility in Chesapeake VA. that had been the old Columbia Yacht sailboat facility. They planned to use it as a coal storage depot prior to the coal being exported overseas. They then changed their mind and decided to use the facility to overhaul rail cars.

I was sent to review their operation and as a result I developed a good relationship with Stuart Perlman, who was in charge of this operation. It was obvious that there was no synergy between SMA and ACI and it made no sense to even consider this. I made my feelings known to Herman and I also told Stuart that a transaction made no sense between our companies.

I told Stuart that if he was looking for a way to divest then he should consider attempting to do a deal with Tony Welters on a leveraged buy- out. Tony had been an officer at Amtrak, a congressional aide to Senator Javits of New York and a Deputy Secretary of Labor under Elizabeth Dole. Tony was from New York and had graduated from NYU's School of Law.

I told Tony that we weren't going to do a transaction with the Perlman's and that he should talk directly to Stuart. Stuart did work out a transaction with Tony and Tony took control ACI.

Late in 1987 I had a call from Tony wanting to know if I could help him. They were looking at doing business with the Navy. Tony had gotten ACI certified as a minority owned company. The Navy had a contract with a firm in Renovo, Pa. to produce Seasheds for them. A Seashed was a 60.000 pound + steel structure that went into the hull of a ship and held a M1-Tank. It prevented a tank from being tossed around inside the hull of a ship. The previous contractor had gone bankrupt and the Navy was looking for someone to take the contract over.

Because of my experience with government contracting, Tony wanted me to assist him in attempting to pull this off. I worked with his team, attended meetings with the Navy and assisted him in putting a bid together.

In late 1987, I received a call from Tony to tell me that the Navy was giving them a contract and he wanted me to join his team, full time.

Based upon the situation at SMA, I decided that this was an opportunity to make something from the ground floor. Tony was based in Northern Virginia even though the main operation of ACI was in Chesapeake. I would need to relocate to Northern Virginia. After discussing this with Sharon it was decided, why not? I told Tony I was excited to come aboard and that I could start in early January 1988. My title was to be Executive Vice President.

Tony had leased two offices in a suite in Arlington, VA. across from the Courthouse Metro stop. In essence, it was similar to WeWorks' offices except these were separate offices with common secretarial, telephone and office services. We didn't know when we were going to move from Virginia Beach.

Scott had finished high school in Roxboro and was attending a local community college in Virginia Beach. Stacy was still in high school and Robin was running her own leased stable in Virginia Beach, having graduated from the University of North Carolina – Chapel Hill in 1984.

I found an apartment in Crystal City, VA. and rented it. My plan was to stay there during the week and go back to Virginia Beach on the week-end until we made the final move.

The first order of business was to determine how we were going to operate two lines of business 500 miles apart. The rail overhaul business wasn't growing. Newport News Shipyards had invested in it in order to determine whether this was a product line that they might decide to pursue in the future. We decided that the Seasheds were probably the line of business that we should concentrate on. Eventually, the Chesapeake Operation was closed and the facility transferred to Newport News Shipbuilding.

I was familiar with Renova, Pa., as it was not far from where I grew up in Clearfield, Pa. The Pennsylvania Railroad had an old facility in Renovo and that was where the Seasheds were being produced.

My Grandfather Shope had dumped a number of coal filled railcars in the Sesquehanna River at Renovo, in an accident, in the 1960's, prior to his retirement.

Renovo is a small community north of Lock Haven, Pa. After the Seashed's were assembled in Renovo they were carried by truck to Perryville, MD where the two halves were connected and then put on a barge to be delivered to Bayone, New Jersey.

Since the previous contractor was in bankruptcy, we needed to put a program together that would give us control of the facility in Renovo and obtain the rights to the equipment and materials that were there. We also needed to assemble a work force and a work plan.

Tony had been friends in school with Edgar Rios. Edgar had graduated from Princeton and Columbia Law School and was an attorney in private practice in Los Angeles specializing in bankruptcy. Edgar flew out and put together a plan to get the property, materials and equipment out of bankruptcy.

We then interviewed the previous work force and were able to put together the labor force needed to move forward. Wayne Keene had been in charge of the workforce under the previous company. Wayne was an old railroader, who I found out later, had actually worked for my father when he was a foreman at the New York Central facility in Jersey Shore, Pa. This line of the NYC railroad started in Cherry Tree, Pa., then went to Clearfield, through Renovo to Jersey Shore and then to Williamsport, following the river, carrying coal from the Central Pa. coal mines.

We needed to put together a finance organization, computer system and administration organization. I found a software package that met the government's requirements but it ran on a Wang Computer System. We determined that it could be connected to Renovo by a dedicated telephone line from Arlington. It also had messaging capability. Today it is called "email." We made arrangements to take about 5,000 square feet of office space in the same building that we had rented the two offices.

We also took advantage of Bea's (Tony's wife) purchasing power through IBM, her employer, and purchased two personal computers with VISICAL and Word Perfect software.

I hired two folks that had worked for me at SMA to help get us started, knowing that they were happy to get out of that environment and realizing that this was an interim position.

Being a small business, we needed to be sure that we could expedite payments from the Navy as rapidly as possible. I went to the disbursing office in Philadelphia and found the person that would be handling payments on our account. The disbursing office was located in a large warehouse building, with hundreds of cubicles. You found someone by the number that was on a post near them.

I found the person that would be handling our payments and I worked out a system where we would hand deliver invoices and she agreed to process them as soon as possible. This system allowed us to get paid within 7 to 10 days from when we delivered the Seashed's to the Navy. This system allowed us to get paid quicker without using progress payments.

Our computer system was installed and worked as promised. We made weekly trips to Renovo to review progress. We started by renting a van that was outfitted with Captain's chairs, a table and seating for 5 plus a driver. We had a driver, Ted Wright. Ted filled many jobs and was essential to our getting things done. We would leave about 5:30 in the morning from Arlington and arrive in Renovo about 10:00. We met until about 4:00 P.M. with lunch brought in. and we arrived back in Arlington about 8:30 or 9:00 at night. We did this weekly. It made a positive difference in the morale of the folks at Renovo and our operation.

On one of our trips, we were on I-70 outside of Frederick, MD when I saw a tire roll past us on the outside. I said look someone lost a tire. That someone was us. Ted was able to get us off to the side of the road without a mishap. After that we decided to see what a new van would cost. We found one for about $25,000 and decided that this was an investment that would pay for itself.

As the Renovo operation continued to operate efficiently, we decided to start to look to other opportunities. We received a follow on order for Seashed's and we then found that the Coast Guard was looking for a contractor to produce buoys. We were able to obtain a contract for buoys and proceeded to add them to the product mix. Our Renova operation consisted mostly of large metal products that required welding to produce.

We also obtained a contract from the army to make floating, pontoon bridges. We also received a contract from the Army to produce ammunition containers. These were very similar to ocean going containers but only 20 feet long.

We had established a relationship with the Director of the Small Business Administration. We were one of a very few SBA Contractors doing the type of work we did. As a result, he was leading an SBA trip in the summer of 1988 to South Korea, Taiwan, Hong Kong and Singapore and it was decided that we were at a stage where Tony and I could take two weeks and go on that trip. We would be visiting manufacturing facilities in each of those countries. The total trip was scheduled to last two weeks.

We had to decide how we would continue to be in contact with our folks at home. Tony found a satellite phone and brought it with him. Cell phones were not portable at this point and no personal computers were allowed to be taken out of the country. The technology explosion was on the horizon.

Visas had to be obtained, vaccinations had to be updated and malaria pills obtained. Approximately 8-10 of us were to go on this trip from various other small businesses. Having never been to the Far East, this was a trip of a lifetime.

It was early summer when we left. We flew from Washington, D.C. to Portland Oregon and then on to Seoul, South Korea. It took over 24 actual hours from when we left to when we arrived in Seoul. We checked in to our hotel and it was recommended that we should take a sauna at the hotel health club. This would help with the Jet lag.

We went to the health club and sat in a bath that had a poison sign on it. It was radon. We then went into a steam bath and after we had our skin scrapped with a towel by one of the attendants. The final was a foot massage. It started out like a normal massage and then the attendant stood on your back and used her feet to massage you. By the time we were finished you felt as though you had gone 10 rounds with Joe Louis.

The next day we went to a facility that was producing Personal Computers (PC's) for IBM, Dell and Acer. Three lines, running parallel with common parts, but different cases. We met with some of the company's engineers and I was surprised when I saw, hanging on their wall, college graduate certificates from MIT, Cal Tech, University of Chicago, etc. with degrees in Electrical Engineering and Computer Science.

They didn't need our computers to reverse engineer them. They had sent their best and brightest to school here in the states and they had taken that engineering knowledge back to their homeland.

When we went to the airport to go to our next destination, Taiwan, we were stopped a half mile from the terminal and the taxi checked to be sure that there were no bombs anywhere. When we arrived at the terminal, sniffer wands were put into our luggage to be sure that no explosives were being carried.

As we stepped into the terminal, all batteries were confiscated. There was a box approximately 4 feet x 4 feet x 4 feet, filled with all types of batteries. The 1988 Olympics were being held in South Korea and this was the beginning of security leading up to them.

After arriving in Taiwan, we checked into our hotel and decided to take a walk. Here we found live animals for sale, snakes, and all types of meat. We also found an open air barbecue shop where barbacue was cooked on large wok type stainless steel containers at least 6 feet in diameter. We decided to sample the barbecue and it was very good. The next morning we visited two plants. One was assembling personal computers and another was producing shipping containers for ocean vessels. We were producing a similar container for the Army to ship ammunition.

The containers were being made by Evergreen Shipping for their ships. The containers were approximately 8 feet by 7 feet by 40 feet and were completely assembled by robots. The entire production line was automated, including painting. They were producing over one container an hour from start to finish at a fraction of the cost that we were incurring. We were told that an automated production line cost approximately $4-5 million to set up.

That evening we had dinner with Mr. "Celanese" of Taiwan. The SBA Administrator, Bob Miller, had known him before. We were entertained at their headquarters. It was an enjoyable evening and we learned a lot about trade between Taiwan and China. Most of their factories were located on the mainland of China but not many people understand that trade had been going on between China and Taiwan for years.

The following day we left for the final stop on our trip, Hong Kong. We flew over Viet Nam on the way but it was impossible to see anything because of the tree coverage. It was obvious why our military used "Agent Orange" during the Viet Nam War.

Arriving in Hong Kong, the landing was between high rise apartments on both sides of the runway. The sky line was incredible. We checked into our hotel on the main land and went to a dinner on a ship in the harbor that could seat over 3,000. All the food was Sichuan style. We were told that this meant that it must be live before cooking. We picked out the fish and seafood from containers on the ship and these were cooked specifically for us. This was an unusual experience but again a new experience.

The next day we went to the "New Territory" to visit some plants where circuit boards were being made and where cell phones were being made. We were actually in China but these factories had been producing goods for years that were stamped "Made in Hong Kong" when they were really made on the main land. The computer circuit boards were being stamped and populated by hand while the employees were wearing sandals and walking around areas where chemicals were on the floor. Obviously OSHA would not have allowed this. Cell phones were being assembled by young women sitting shoulder to shoulder. A competitive advantage compared to the USA.

One day we were entertained at a lunch put on by Cathay Pacific. I sat next to the Managing Director who was from the United Kingdom. He indicated that this was the best assignment he had ever had. When he would return to England for vacation his family and friends would feel so bad because of his assignment. He said he didn't tell them any different.

We also visited with an American Law Firm in Hong Kong. It was interesting getting their perspective on the area. We had the opportunity to do some shopping, including purchasing some custom made clothes that were ready in two days. The price was right as was the quality.

In summary, the venture to the Far East was eye opening and extremely interesting. It gave one a different perspective on the trade policies of the US.

On the way home we flew to Hawaii via Japan where we met our wives and spent a few days of R&R.

Back in the states, we looked at our business in a totally different light. It was obvious that we could never be competitive in the heavy metal manufacturing arena.

We decided to look at what other areas within the government contracting arena that we could exploit. We had made contact with Dan Johnston out of Durham, N.C. when we were setting up our computer system for our heavy metal manufacturing operation.

Dan had completed all but his dissertation at UNC-Chapel Hill for a Doctorate in Computer Science. He had some contacts at E.P.A. in the Research Triangle Park. They were going to be going out for bid for a systems integrator for personal computers. We decided to look at the requirements and brought Dan on board to head that effort.

The contract required a facility in the Research Park to assemble computers as required by the E.P.A. It was estimated to be at least $200 million a year in business and would be a multi-year contract.

We assembled a team, put a bid together and established a new corporation, Atlantic Systems Incorporated to bid on this contract. We were successful. It was estimated that the contract could be worth as much as $1 Billion. We decided that this was our way out of the heavy metal manufacturing business.

Scott - Air Force

Stacy Graduation - Virginia Wesleyan University

Chapter Seventeen

About the same time in late 1988 we learned that the Commonwealth of Pennsylvania was going to go out for bid on a contract to manage about 80,000 Medicaid individuals in the Philadelphia area. This was to be a follow on contract to a Medicaid Managed Care Demonstration Program. The previous contractor had gone bankrupt and the Commonwealth was looking for a new contract.

We had no health care experience but we were successful in understanding and operating government contracts so we decided to look at the process. The traditional Medicaid program was a fee for service program with the state paying providers for services rendered on a fee basis. The state wanted to mitigate their risk and wanted to contract with a third person on a per capital basis to operate the program and transfer the risk to that person.

As we assembled a team to review the contract bid process, we decided that we could offer the computer system as our segment of expertise and be a subcontractor to someone else. We had a consultant that was assisting us in our ACI work, former US Navy Admiral, Gene Grinstead. He introduced us to Perot Systems. They had been doing much of the Medicaid processing for states.

We teamed up with them and attended the pre-bidders conference in Harrisburg. After that conference we began to analyze the cost data that the state gave to all bidders. The state was looking for a cost per capita or in essence a fixed price bid based upon an estimated number of recipients.

As this analysis was being reviewed, Perot Systems advised us that they were not going to follow through on their bidding. If we wanted to proceed, we would have to bid on the program ourself. We reviewed where we were and decided to approach a local healthcare consulting company. They were consultants in the healthcare world and had a computer system that was supposed to be able to handle claims, etc.

We met with them and they decided that they would team with us but that they did not want to be the primary bidder, as it was too risky. We regrouped and found a primary care provider in the Philadelphia area that was mainly treating the Medicaid population, Lomax & Associates. Walter Lomax was a physician and had a number of offices in the area.

We put together a team with Atlantic Systems Incorporated in the lead with Lomax and the consulting firm as participants.

We looked at the claim information and found that over 60% of the cost was from inpatient services. If we could control hospitalizations we would be controlling the major cost driver. We had to have contracts with all of the major hospitals in the Philadelphia area, primary and specialty physicians and pharmacies. This was a herculean task. In addition, we had to prove financial stability. To do this we decided to use reinsurance. This was expensive but it was the only way to demonstrate financial viability. We were able to convince Lloyd's of London, through the Jardine Company as broker, to reinsure our costs. Our reinsurance premium was $3 million for $10 million of coverage but it also included a no claims bonus or a rebate.

We created a new company to bid on the contract, "Healthcare Management Alternatives (HMA). Our bid to the state was to be based upon a % of fee for service. As we put our numbers together we came to a fee for service number of 92%. Our consulting company indicated that they could not support our bid because no one had been able to operate at that rate in the past.

They would only agree to support us at 95% of FFS. We decided to submit our bid at 92% because we felt quite comfortable at that rate. This was a competitive bid and having experience in government contracting, we knew that we had to have a good technical proposal as well as the lowest cost if we were to be successful.

In March/April 1989 we found out we were the lowest bidder. Originally, the winner was to have 6 months to be up and running, however the state announced that unless we could be operational by July 1, 1989 there would be no contract. In essence we had 45 days to obtain all the network providers, set up our office complex, put our computer system together and hire approximately 90 people.

We also needed to raise $3 million in order to show the Commonwealth of Pennsylvania that we were financially viable. Fortunately, I had a relationship with a banker at American Security and Trust in Washington, D.C. She went to bat for us based upon the contract with Pennsylvania. She was able to get us a $3 million loan with Tony, Edgar and I signing a demand note and with our wives also signing .This was a stretch but we all agreed.

We immediately went to work with a matrix of what needed to be done and a time line for each event. Tony worked on getting the hospitals signed up, Edgar the pharmacies and I went to work on getting the facility set up and the personnel hired. Tony's wife, Bea, still worked for IBM and she assisted in getting the computer system set up and operational. We had 45 days to make this happen and we achieved our objective. The day before we were to go live, the Secretary of Health for Pennsylvania, John White, visited our facility to determine whether they were going to sign the contract. They found us compliant and signed the contract.

Not having any healthcare experience was actually a positive instead of a negative as we had no preconceived idea as to what could or could not be done. When we were initially announced as the winners of the contract, we assembled a group of healthcare professionals that Tony & Edgar knew from their days in college. These were Doctors, nurses, and administrators. We took them on a retreat to the Island of St. Martens as a reward for helping us understand the healthcare system. The purpose of the retreat was to discuss all of the good and bad in the Medicaid system and how best to manage this population to achieve the best health outcomes at the lowest cost.

This retreat allowed us to think outside of the box and be original in going forward.

One of the things that we found was that claims for a particular month took about 6 months to be completely paid out. As a result there was a significant cash build up. Lag schedules were utilized to determine medical cost. This was where you showed on a monthly basis claims submitted and claims paid. Trends could be developed as a result. Data was critical in the analysis of how one was doing.

We had limitations imposed by the state as to what we could invest our cash in. Generally it had to be Class A/B bonds and nothing speculative. As an example, if you had 80,000 members and you received a capitation check monthly of $250 per member per month, then you would be receiving $20 million monthly.

If you estimated medical expense at 92% then you would take 8% of that amount for your administration and profit or $1.6 million. That could be transferred to the company cash account and the remaining $18.4 million would be set aside for medical expenses. If based on the lag schedules, you paid out 10% the first month, 15% the second 20 % the third etc. You can see how cash would build up.

Most health insurance companies stretch their payments to their providers over as long a period as possible, we decided to accelerate payments to within 30 days of receipt of a claim. The reasoning was that the amount of interest that we could earn was minimal and we decided that the good will that we could earn by paying the providers timely was worth more. We were right.

By the end of the first six months we had a build- up in cash for claims of over $25 million and we were able to pay back our $3 million loan and were debt free. We were also operating at a lower medical cost ratio then we had anticipated.

During this period we were no longer operating ACI in Chesapeake. Newport Shipbuilding had taken over the facility in lieu of repayment of the loan they had made to ACI.

The Renovo operation was still operating producing Buoys for the Coast Guard and ammunition containers for the army. The EPA computer system integration contract was going well and we had bid on a follow on program that could be worth up to $1 Billion over 5 years. However there was a major issue brewing. We learned that the EPA's Inspector General (IG) was investigating us for fraud. Supposedly, our manager of that facility had established another company and was going to supply some of the items we were to supply to E.P.A., to us, at a mark-up or in essence double dealing. We had to put him on administrative leave and hire a law firm to defend us against these claims. After about 6 months and $700,000 in legal expenses we agreed to forfeit our contract, turn our facility in Renovo over to the government in return for a non- prosecution agreement and relinquish our E.P.A. contract. I was in favor of fighting the claims but my partners thought this was the best for the company as we were allowed to continue our healthcare operation.

The E.P.A. Inspector General's office had brought a lawsuit against our manager but lost in court. Although the manager had discussed setting up a company to do what the government had claimed, he never did and the government was not harmed. An expensive lesson because we had to relinquish our Renovo operation and the E.P.A. contract.

The balance of 1989 was a busy time. We were in Philadelphia at least two days a week while we were battling with the government over the EPA Contract.

Toward the balance of 1989, the Commonwealth of Pa. had received a protest that our contract was not won fairly. We had many meetings with Pennsylvania. We agreed that we would be willing to open the contract to a rebid. They did and we were again successful winning the contract and we continued to build a healthcare business.

We learned that New Jersey was going to sell their Medicaid Program to a private insurer. We decided to look at the possibility of developing a Medicaid managed care business there and entered a bid for the Medicaid recipients. We were successful and set up the New Jersey operation in offices in Newark.

We learned that New York was going to contract out their Medicaid program in Brooklyn and we decided that we would bid on that also. We were again successful and set up offices in lower Manhattan for the New York operation.

As we started operations in New Jersey and New York, we realized that our computer system in Pa. was not going to be adequate to operate an expanded program. We learned about a software company in Phoenix, AZ that had a Medicaid oriented software package that could manage our medical program. We did not need to have our own computer system as we would be using this system on a network basis and pay based upon a per member per month charge.

We contracted with INC and found that the system was manageable without us having a large IT staff. We also contracted with INC to do claims processing for us.

In a short period of time we had become the go to company for Medicaid Managed Care and we were profitable from day 1. Our members were receiving quality healthcare at a lower cost per member per month than what we were paying for our own employees.

We continued to use reinsurance as a safety net though it was becoming expensive since we never had any claims. When New York was started, we decided to have discussions with CNN Insurance out of Chicago about being a financial partner. We had the finances to go it alone but we thought that there would be some advantages to having CNN Insurance as a partner.

We went to Chicago and meet with their executives to determine whether we could reach an agreement. Tony, Edgar, Andre Dugan and I went. We were going to ask for $3 million for 20% of the business but after the discussions began it appeared to me that they might be willing to invest more for the same percentage.

When the moment was correct I told them that we were looking for $6 million for 20%. The rest of our team thought I had lost my mine and they decided that it was time for them to exit and go home. It was decided that I would stay and see if I could work out a transaction. By the end of the day CNN agreed to invest $6 million in our New York operation.

We utilized our Philadelphia model in New Jersey and New York. Our New Jersey cost of acquiring the Medicaid program was a little over $20 million. We were able to borrow that from our bank.

As we continued to grow it was obvious that it might make sense to see if we could purchase the Arizona Company, INC. This would give us a technology platform to support all of our Medicaid Plans. I had a discussion with the founder of INC and after a number of meetings we were able to reach an agreement to purchase them. As part of the deal, we would bring in our own management team.

We decided that we needed to put all of our Healthcare entities under one parent company so "AmeriChoice Corporation" was established.

Our next acquisition was the Medicaid Program in Michigan. It was owned by a private equity company who wanted to sell. We reviewed the program and were able to reach an agreement to purchase that membership. We were now operating in Pa., NJ, NY, and Michigan with our technology platform in Arizona.

I believe it was sometime in 1995 that I received a phone call from someone who said they were with TA Associates, a large private equity firm based in Boston. They wanted to know if we had any interest in selling our firm. I got their information and said I would get back to them. I told Tony and Edgar about the call and then we did some checking to see if they were a legitimate organization.

Everything checked out and we set up a meeting to talk to them. We met with their healthcare partner, Bob Daley, and it was obvious that they really wanted to own a piece of us. They usually invested by having a preferential stock. We said that we were open to an investment but that they would not have a preferential position. An agreement was reached and we sold them, I believe, 20% based upon an agreed upon valuation.

On September 11, 2001, I was just leaving a fitness center in Northern Virginia to go to our headquarters in Tyson Corner when a radio announcement said that a plane had just crashed into the World Trade Center building in New York City. Our New York office was just a few blocks from that location. We had over 200 employees there. As soon as I arrived at our headquarters, I found everyone gathered in the conference room watching this tragedy unfold on television.

We tried to contact our New York office but were not able to get through.

When we were finally able to reach one of the managers via cell phone, we heard that everyone was evacuated and safe. It was a few weeks before we were able to gain entrance to our New York office but fortunately our New Jersey office, in Newark, was able to handle our New York work load temporarily.

I felt fortunate that we had escaped this tragedy until I saw that another plane had crashed into the Pentagon. My cousin Jane's husband, John McDonald, was an Asst. Secretary of the Army, and where the plane crashed was where his office was. It took a while but we finally received the news that he was ok as he was out of the building for a meeting. Sadly, a number of his staff were not as lucky. A terrible day all around.

We had developed a diverse management team at each of the operations and a small central headquarters organization. Our revenues were now approaching $1 Billion and our profits were averaging 5% after taxes. We were now operating in 5 states with over 1,000 employees. In addition all of our plans were profitable. We realized that we needed financing to continue to expand. There were also now three new competitors in the space that were investor financed. It was time to consider whether a public offering might be the next step in our growth.

We decided to test the waters and met with a number of the major Wall Street investment firms. After a review of the market we decided to retain Bank of America's investment group to do a public offering. We prepared an S-1 and were in the process of submitting it to the SEC when we were advised by Bank of America that the United Healthcare Group was interested in meeting with us to discuss an acquisition.

We met with their C.O.O., Stephen Hemsley and his acquisition team. They made an offer to purchase our company with the condition that Edgar, Tony and I would agree to continue as an employee for 3 to 5 years.

The purpose of the acquisition was to combine their Medicaid business with ours and assign the management to us with the objective of making their Medicaid business as profitable as ours. We agreed to accept their offer and we finalized the transaction in October of 2002.

I had a contract to stay until October of 2005. However the longer I stayed the more panful it was. I was finally able to leave in May 2005. They were a successful company but very bureaucratic.

From January 1988 until October 2002, we developed a company that was "color blind" and had become very successful. We were a diverse company of men, women, ethnicities, religions, etc. The founders were African-American, Latino and Caucasian. The founders were also all first generation college graduates. We hired the best people we could find for the position regardless of their color, religion or national origin. As a result we were a rainbow. I have to laugh today when I see companies still struggling to create a diverse employment base. It starts at the top and isn't as difficult as many organizations make it.

It wasn't easy but it was worth the pain and agony. I am sometimes sorry that we sold to United because I think about all the good we could have continued doing.

Edgar stayed with United for a short period after I left and Tony continued for over 10 years with United in their Corporate Management Team. I was happy to leave as it was painful being there.

Anthony(Tony)Welters, Dr.Walter Lomax,Boris Shapiro, Edgar
Rios, A.J. Henley, Jess sweely

Chapter Eighteen
Sweely Family Foundation:

In the 1990's, I set up the "Sweely Family Foundation" for the purpose of the family's charitable giving program. I primarily wanted to provide an annual scholarship for a graduate of Clearfield Senior High School in Clearfield, Pa. The conditions were that the recipient needed financial aid, be in the top 10% of the class and go to a college or university outside Pennsylvania. The scholarship would amount to $40,000 at $10,000 a year for a period of over 4 years.

The purpose of the last condition was so that the person selected could experience a more diverse environment then what was in rural Pennsylvania. I wanted them to see that there was a whole new world waiting.

I set up a scholarship committee, chaired by my cousin, Nancy Sweely Fink, with the members selected by her. I had no control over who was selected.

The Pittsburgh Foundation in Pittsburgh, Pa. was selected to administer the scholarship. I contacted the administration of the high school to advise them what I planned to do and ask for their assistance in promoting the scholarship. I must say that I was disappointed by their response. They were not enthusiastic at all at my plan.

I decided to go ahead anyway and I was able to get a piece in the local paper about the scholarship. The first year we had about 6 applicants. The young woman selected was admitted to Cornell University but needed financial support.

The following year we had approximately the same number of applicants and this time a young man who had been admitted to Cornell also was selected.

We continued to have about the same number of applicants over the next few years. Those selected went to St. John's in Maryland, Liberty University, and Long Island University among others. They all graduated in 4 years.

As time went on, we found that the number of applicants dwindled. We were only getting 3 or four applicants and then we only received two with one not financially needy.

I contacted the Pittsburgh Foundation to discuss what they were seeing with respect to the other scholarships that they managed. They told me that they weren't getting any applicants for many of the scholarships that they managed.

They indicated that the young folks of today couldn't be bothered to fill out scholarship applications.

After careful consideration I decided to drop the scholarship because there just wasn't any interest. When I graduated in 1956 we had about 226 in my senior class, with 51 taking college preparatory classes.

There were now less than 150 in the senior class. I was hopeful that we would have been able to continue but it just wasn't to be.

Chapter Nineteen
Farm Employees

In 1990, we acquired land in Madison, VA. and went about constructing a family horse farm. The first phase was completed in 1991. Finding employees was now the difficult issue. I was informed that there were organizations that assisted in finding individuals in Europe that wanted to come to the United States and work. There was a J-1 Visa that allowed them to come here for 6 months and then extend for another 6 months.

I contacted one of the organizations and they said that they had a number of young people from Ireland and the United Kingdom that wanted to come to the United States and that they had horse experience.

I said that we would like to try the program. We needed to provide housing and a living wage and transportation. Our first employees were from Ireland and were young and hardworking individuals. We continued to use this program and over the next few years we had individuals from Germany, France, Estonia, South Africa and Lithuania come to work at the farm. They all spoke multiple languages, including English and were devoted to their craft.

A few years after the European Union was established in November of 1993, we saw fewer and fewer applicants wanting to come to the United States as they were now able to travel and work in most of the E.U. countries.

We had two outstanding young individuals, one from South Africa and one from Estonia, who appeared to have future potential. Glunke was from South Africa and Pirit was from Estonia. I asked them what their plans were when the returned home. Both said that they would like to go to college if they could afford it. I asked them if they could get in college in the United States would they want to go. It was a resounding "yes" from both.

I said that if they were accepted to a college we would support them and pay the college costs. I told them that they would need to take the SAT's and apply to a college of their choosing.

Perit choose George Mason University. She scored almost 1200 on her SAT's, without a coaching course, and was accepted immediately. She chose International Affairs as her major and graduated in 4 years. Her folks were able to come to her graduation and were extremely proud. She considered going to Law School but returned to Estonia and is working for the government.

Glunke always wanted to be a veterinarian and she decided on Colorado State University because they had both a pre-vet program and a veterinary school. She also scored almost 1200 on her SAT's, without taking a coaching course, and was accepted also. She was on track to graduate in three years but I told her that she needed to slow down. She graduated in 3 ½ years without going to summer school.

He folks were not able to come to her graduation but were also very proud of her success.

She had applied to three vet schools, Colorado State, Virginia Tech and Oregon State. She was wait-listed on the first two but accepted at Oregon State. We told her that we would continue to support her dream and she enrolled.

Between graduating and enrolling at Oregon State she managed to make a trip home to South Africa to see her parents. She reconnected with a former boyfriend and they carried on a long distant relationship her first year at Oregon State.

She decided to see if she could transfer to the veterinary school at Pretoria, South Africa. Surprisingly, she was accepted. No one had ever successfully transferred in before. She returned home and completed her veterinary school work in South Africa and became a successful veterinarian.

The relationship ended but she found her soul mate while at school and is now happily married and has just moved to Ontario, Canada with her husband and children.

I am so proud to have been able to give both a new beginning.

From 1991 through 2000, we had over a dozen young men and women from Ireland, England, Lithuania, Latvia, France, Germany and South Africa work at the farm on a J-1 Visa for anywhere from 6 months to a year. They all were energetic, hard-working, competent and spoke multiple languages. They were happy for the opportunity and it appeared that they were more mature then our young people.

We were successful in helping at least 8 receive their "Green Cards" and go on to a productive life here in the States. The establishment of the European Economic Union (EEU) and the increasing difficulty of obtaining a J-1 Visa changed this program. Young folks from EEU countries could now obtain jobs in other EEU countries with little or no difficulty.

Glunke's Graduation -2008 -Marcie Siegel, Jess, Glunke, Sharon

Robin -Showjumping

Acorn Hill SteepleChasing

Acorn Hill Homebred Racing

Chapter Twenty
The After Life

The next question was what now? I had turned 67 in May of 2005 but I wasn't ready to stop just yet.

In 1990, Robin was pursuing her horse career and we were renting a barn in Virginia Beach. Scott was in the Air Force, flying AWACS missions around the world and stationed in Japan. Stacy was pursuing her college degree at Virginia Wesleyan University in Virginia Beach, VA. Sharon and I decided that we would look for a farm closer to where we were living, Oakton, VA in Northern Virginia .Sharon was selling real estate for Long and Foster in Northern, VA so she took on the task of looking for property.

In her research, she found some land for sale in Madison, VA. Madison was about two hours from Oakton and a half hour from Charlottesville, VA., home to the University of Virginia. We decided to look and were pleasantly pleased with what we found. 85 acres of open land that would lend itself to developing a horse farm and even the possibility of a retirement home for us.

We were successful in reaching agreement with the owner and proceeded to call our friend and architect, Bill Bowling. Bill was working for himself outside of Roanoke. We met with Bill and indicated that we wanted to develop a master plan so that we would know how everything might fit since we didn't plan to build everything at once.

Bill put together a plan, based upon our discussions. It included a home for Robin, an indoor riding arena, barn, shop and cottage for us. This still left room for a retirement house later. We were in agreement and started the process of Bill developing plans for those buildings.

In the meantime, we started to look for builders. We selected Bruce Bowman to build the residential structures and P.J. Williams to do the barns, indoor arena, shop and run-in sheds.

Because this was a massive project and something that neither was particularly accustomed to we went with cost plus contracts. It worked well for both of us.

Construction was finished in 1991 and Robin moved from Virginia Beach. We would spend the week-ends in the cottage. As Robin got more involved with the horses and competing nationally as well as internationally we needed to expand the facility. We added two apartments for farm help and a run in shed. We traveled to Ireland and Germany to look at horses and started to buy young horses in both locations. We left some there with breeders and brought some home. We also developed a friendship with many in the horse industry throughout Europe.

At home, I became interested in race horses and started a breeding program of thoroughbred horses. I also became interested in Steeple Chasing and started purchasing a number of horses for that venue. Jack Fisher became our trainer.

Don Litz became our advisor on the thoroughbred breeding side. Both were competent and highly successful.

Robin started to spend more time in Europe, riding on the European circuit. Our spare time was spent traveling there.

As we started to breed our own sport horses and race horses, we decided to build a breeding barn and another shop on the rear of the property. This was where we also planned our retirement home. Bill was contracted to develop the breeding barn and we completed that in about 1994-95. In 2000 we decided to design our retirement home. After many versions we finally settled on the design and completed the process around 2002. I also decided that I wanted a separate building for a home office. That was completed around 2002 also. What a project.

In 2002, Sharon said that a tract of land, 295 acres, was going to be for sale just off Rt. 29 on Wolftown Road. She thought that we might want to consider adding it to our portfolio. I said we would look at it but I wasn't particularly interested. We received a plat and decided to drive over as much as we could in our 4 wheel drive vehicle. It had a long road frontage and was well proportioned and was actually a very nice piece of property.

We discussed it and decided to make an offer. We agreed on one condition, if we could purchase it I could plant some wine grapes. I had been following the wine industry in Virginia and felt that there was an opportunity.

We were successful in acquiring the property and decided to look seriously at what would be required to make growing grapes a viable business.

We had set up a Family Home Office in 2002 to handle the family investments and I had hired Marcie Siegal to run the office. Marcie had previously worked at

SMA when I was there and I knew that she was the right person for the job.

We decided to look into the Virginia wine industry in more detail and hired Gabrielle Rausse to be a consultant. He had been involved in establishing the Barboursville Winery some 20 some years before for the Zonin family of Italy. Gabrielle suggested that we needed to find a winemaker as our first step.

He suggested a number of possibilities and we decided on Frantz Ventre, a winemaker at Jefferson Winery in Charlottesville. Frantz was French and had been educated in France and was considered an up and coming star.

The first thing that we did was visit a number of Virginia wineries and then we decided to make a trip to California to visit a number of California wineries. The management at these wineries was very open and forthcoming of the good and the bad. We were particularly interested in the growing of the fruit and the winery operations. We then decided that we should visit some of the wineries in France. Frantz was delegated to put together a trip where we would be able to see the wine making process at both small and large wineries.

We went to France and visited a number of vineyards in the Bordeaux and St. Emilion regions. The owners were very forthcoming. Now it was time for us to develop our own winery.

With that behind us we also needed to hire a vineyard manager and after a number of interviews we decided on Oliver Asberger, a German vineyard manager.

With the basic staff in place it was now time to consider how to convert our 295 acres into a new Virginia Winery. We decided to name it Acorn Hill Winery. We would later change the name to "Sweely Estate Winery" to avoid a conflict with a winery in

California. I placed a call to Bill Bowling, an architect and family friend in Roanoke. Bill had designed our horse farm and main home and we had been friends for over 30 years.

Bill said he had no experience designing a winery but he would act as the architect in charge and recommended that we use his former firm, Hayes, Seay, Mattern & Mattern to do all of the detail work.

We met and laid out our objectives and decided that the best approach would be to arrange a trip to California where they would be able to meet with some of the folks that we met with to understand the wine making process. That was arraigned and we also began putting a business plan together. Our objective was to limit our investment to about $9 to $10 million and try to get to about 25,000 cases of production within five years. Most of the wineries in Virginia were small, 3 to 5,000 cases but there were 3 or 4 that were in the 25 to 35,000 cases.

As we started looking at financial data it became clear that at 5,000 cases we could not become profitable. Around 15,000 would break even and at 25,000 we could become profitable and self- sustaining.

We settled on a design for the winery production facility and let a contract to Martin Brothers, a firm out of Roanoke, VA. In the meantime we prepared the vineyard ground and planted the initial grape vines. We estimated that it would take two to three years to have a meaningful harvest.

We built a small building to store equipment and until the production facility was completed. We used it to make small batches of wine from our own grapes.

We finished the production building in early 2007 and installed the tanks that we purchased in France. This was a very modern facility and was equal to anything in

California. At the same time we contracted with the architectural firm to design a tasting facility and conference/wedding center. The production facility cost us over $8 million and the estimate for the tasting facility was another $9 million. This was over our budget but we knew that this facility would add significant value to the entire operation.

The question now was how to finance the rest of the project. We gave the go ahead to the contractor and reviewed options for the funding needed. This was in the middle of the recession of 2007-2009.

We were approached by a representative from SunTrust Bank and after talks with a number of their representatives, they agreed to provide us with approximately $18 million in financing.

We completed the tasting facility, approximately 20,000 square feet, including a full commercial kitchen, private rooms and a conference room that would hold 200 that could be used as a wedding venue.

We were off and running. We planted additional vines and we now had acreage that could sustain a minimum of 10,000 cases annually. We established a marketing program and we were now in business.

In 2009, SunTrust was experiencing financial issues internally because of the recession and they called our loan. I attempted to find investors but to no avail because of the economy. We battled for almost a year and finally ended up selling the winery to Steve Case of AOL fame for 50 cents on a dollar. Our dream was now over and we were now in survivor mode. We were left with the family farm in Madison and nothing else.

We converted the farm into a boarding and training facility and attempted to stay afloat. In January of 2008, I was diagnosed with Hodgkins Lymphoma and underwent eight months of chemo at the University of Virginia's Cancer Center. In August of 2008 they determined that I was in recession and needed only follow up. To this day I am still in recession.

I was born with a bi-cuspid aortic valve (two flaps instead of three). This was found during an annual physical at the Mayo Clinic in Scottdale, AZ. I was told that I would eventually have to have it replaced and that I would know when that time was. I had been followed by Dr. Craddock of the Cardiology Department at UVA Health and in April 2012 I was becoming short of breath. Upon examination it was determined that the valve needed replaced and it was scheduled for early May.

I had open heart surgery and the valve was replaced with a Bovine Valve. I was told that everything went well and that I needed Cardiac Rehab. I completed that and I felt as good as ever. It was estimated that the valve should be good for approximately 15 years. I was to have annual appointments with a cardiologist.

During this same time period Sharon fell trying to lead a horse to pasture and broke her leg in a number of places. The recovery was a long process but all went well. Again, "getting old is not for the faint of heart."

Entrance -Acorn Hill Farm

Acorn Hill Home Office

Acorn Hill Vineyard

Acorn Hill Production facility

Acorn Hill Winery - First Harvest

Acorn Hill Farm Winery Hospitality Center

Guinness - Dublin, Ireland

Thomas Wolfangel - Irish Friend

Cliffs of Mohr - Ireland

Budapest, Hungary

Manfred AllWorden-German Friend

Jess & Detlef Saul (Horse Breeder) -Germany

Valkenswaard, Holland Int'l Horse Show

Monaco Harbor

Paris, France

American cemetery - Normandy, France

Normandy, France Beach

Jess & Sharon - Normandy, France

Normandy, France Beach

Acorn Hill Farm

Acorn Hill Farm Thoroughbred Baby

Acorn Hill Farm Horses in Pasture

Robin, Sharon, Jess, Stacy & Scott

⎯⎯⎯⎯⎯◯◯⎯⎯⎯⎯⎯

Epilogue

It is now 2022 and I am now 84 and Sharon will be 80 in December. We have survived the Covid-19 Epidemic so far and keep ourself busy around the farm. Robin is trying to make a go of boarding and training horses, after a successful International Show Jumping career at South American and European venues, including participating as a member of the United States Equestrian Team. Stacy & her husband Tim are trying to salvage their online business after a devastating two years because of Covid and Scott has recently taken a disability retirement from the Air Force National Guard in Georgia.

Our Granddaughter, Kumi, is in Hawaii, where she received both an undergraduate and graduate degree from the University of Hawaii and is teaching English as a Second Language. Our Grandson, JT, has recently gone to Japan with his mother. That story is still to be heard.

Scott's first daughter, Elizabeth, is married with two children and has a successful career in San Antonio, TX as an accountant with IHeart Radio.

I try to stay busy at my farm office writing, mainly about issues for the family, and helping a few small businesses with their accounting and tax issues.

It has been quite the journey for a small town boy from Central Pennsylvania. Sharon and I have had dinner with Mikhail Gorbachev and attended two

Inauguration Balls. In addition to work, I learned to snow ski, play golf, sail, and raise horses. I certainly made some mistakes along the way but I am not sure I would change anything. I have travelled the world, met interesting people, and had a great life. I have loved every minute of it, the good and the bad. I could not have done it without my wife Sharon. We just celebrated our 61st anniversary.

During my career, I have had the privilege of working for and with some of the best mentor's one could ever hope for. Many were veterans of World War II but you would never know that. They never discussed their war time experiences but they were members of "The Greatest Generation." As a result, they had a perspective on life that appears to have been lost today.

Also, none of this would have been possible without first getting an education.

About the Author

Jess Sweely is a small town boy who found his way to the top of the business world through education and dedication to his work. The first of his family to earn a college degree, he is a graduate of Benjamin Franklin University, American University and George Washington University and a Certified Public Accountant in the District of Columbia.

He and his wife reside on their family farm in Madison, Virginia.